DIY SOS

First published in Great Britain in 2000 by HarperCollins
an imprint of HarperCollins*Publishers*
77–85 Fulham Palace Road
London W6 8JB

www.**fire**and**water**.com

In association with the BBC

Design and picture research: Essential Books
Nick Knowles photography: Laurence Cendrowicz
Interiors photography: Nick Carter

1 3 5 7 9 10 8 6 4 2

Printed and bound in the UK by Scotprint

A catalogue record for this book is available from the British Library

ISBN 0-00-710117-1

Lowri Turner & Nick Knowles

DIY SOS

The book that rescues you from *DIY* disaster!

As seen on
BBC ONE

All images taken from the BBC series *DIY SOS* except those reproduced with kind permission of the DIY Library; various tool images courtesy of Bosch, Draper Tools and Stanley; page 41 World's End Tiles; page 67 Magnet; page 115 Rhode Design Furniture; page 143 Harvey Jones.

The author and publishers have made every reasonable effort to contact all copyright holders. Any errors that may have occurred are inadvertent and anyone who for any reason has not been contacted is invited to write to the publishers so that a full acknowledgement may be made in subsequent editions of this work.

More detailed information on DIY can be found in the *Collins Complete DIY Manual.*

CONTENTS

Introduction

I suppose we should have known it all along. This country and the hammer-wielding, power-tooled maniacs who 'maintain' it were tailormade for *DIY SOS*. Now there were some in the production office in those early days who scoffed at the idea of making a TV series about people who had messed up their own homes so badly that it would require a large group of professional building and decorating experts just to put it right again. 'Ridiculous,' they said 'no-one's ever going to own up to being that bad at DIY.' How wrong can you be? Mind you, even I was surprised by what we actually did find out there...

Hiding behind the manicured lawns and half-drawn curtains of Britain lurks a shadowy underworld of half-finished wallpapering, botched plumbing and catastrophic kitchen fitting. Who does this? We all do. We see an expert on telly, revamping a whole room in a day and we think: 'That looks easy, I'll have a go.' The thing is we don't have the faintest idea what we're doing. I have to admit that I too have had my share of DIY disasters. There was the time I tiled the kitchen really badly. Forever after I had to position the kettle and the toaster to conceal the worst bits. Others endure much worse. We featured one woman in the first series who had no living room floor for nine years because her husband took it up and couldn't put it back down again.

Now for those of you who regularly watch *DIY SOS*, you will realise that dealing with these kind of problems in these kind of homes has given our team a rather unique insight into what goes most wrong, most places, most often. We have become the 'paramedics of DIY'. First to arrive at the scene when some poor unsuspecting house has suffered a nasty internal injury. Once there, like athletes in the blocks, our untiring professionals spring majestically into action. Bob, Brigid, Billy, Chris and Julian from Nick's team and Garfield, Ian Steve and Livi from my team all get stuck in. OK, we do mess about a bit as well.

However, through all of this hard work and hilarity one thing's for sure. If you get the *DIY SOS* team working on your home there's going to be a fantastic result at the end of the day. Or the end of the next day. Or, very occasionally, sometime during the day after that. You see, we took a decision right at the beginning of *DIY SOS* to make it as real as possible. If there's a hitch, it all goes wrong, or we can't finish the job at all, then we show you the grisly truth. Talking of grisly truth, no, I don't have a hair and make-up team, as some viewers suspect. Also, as one parent of a scout we helped in Stalybridge said: 'I thought you only did the work when the cameras

rolled.' We all get stuck in, whether we're filming or not, and I have the paint-splattered Tee-shirts to prove it. Anyway, if anyone knows how to fix up a DIY problem – fix it so that it looks fixed and it stays fixed – then it's got to be us. We've piped, plumbed, plugged, patched, plastered, pasted, papered, painted, and generally perspired up and down the country.

Furthermore, *DIY SOS* is filmed in exactly the amount of time we say on-screen. All the projects are either two- or three-day jobs and that means that whatever brilliant plans or proposals we come up with have to be quick, easy and by and large, pretty inexpensive. We now have some of the best evidence as to what people really want (or have) to tackle when they are maintaining or improving their homes, and some of the best tips and techniques on how you can make those tasks not just feasible, but actually rather fun. The kind of solutions that anyone could successfully apply to the kind of problems that everyone at some time has to face...

'Well,' I hear you say, 'if you really do know so much about something as useful as that, why don't you put it all into a book or something?' And you know what, I think that's a brilliant idea...

Repairs & Improvements

There's no getting around it, houses break. And when they do, you're almost certainly going to know about it. You'll either get wet, cold, plunged into darkness or receive such a stream of complaints from the rest of the family that you have no choice other than to pick up the toolbox or the Yellow Pages to call for help. More importantly, the longer you leave it, the more tools or the more help you're going to need... And if that's not a sobering enough thought, then consider this – most people seem to have an as yet unidentified gene inside them which means that even if they do live in a house which is technically perfect, they will eventually feel an irresistible urge to fiddle about with something in it until it finally does break... However, this needn't be a path which you fear to tread. Far from it. It doesn't take much equipment or time, and it doesn't need a degree in rocket science. All you need is the knowledge and the confidence to get started, which is exactly what this chapter is designed to provide.

'Do you know,' asks Lowri,

'We bumped into one Essex lady whose bathroom didn't have a door — and faced directly down the stairs!'

'the most amazing thing about doing *DIY SOS*?' No, it's not the fact that I can now lay a laminate floor, fill a hole with quick-drying cement and know what a noggin is. It's not even the state that some people get their homes into; it's the look of complete shock on their faces when we turn up to put it right. They may have trashed the living room, dismantled the kitchen or even have removed an entire wall of their house, but they never imagined that their less-than-handy work would now be starring on TV, or that the great British public would have voted to rescue their family from the rubble of their appalling DIY.

Some of the blame must go to TV programmes – not us, of course! – that suggest home improvement is easy. Enthused by what we've seen on the small screen, a lot of us are all too willing to make radical and sometimes devastating changes to our precious homes without any real idea of what we're doing. You'd be amazed how much difference you can make to a perfectly good home with a bit of time on your hands and a sledgehammer. Of course, that change isn't always for the better. An Englishman's home

Garfield, his golden rule: no job is too small; everything is achievable if it's discussed and thought through first.

may still be his castle, but the building has not yet been invented that can withstand an Englishman's urge to DIY... On the first series of *DIY SOS* we featured a lot of male DIY disasters. The sort of bloke who starts papering the spare room, goes down the pub for a quick one and doesn't come back for five years. Perhaps to get their own back, for Series Two we were deluged with tales of women who'd run amok with filler guns, etc.

We bumped into one Essex lady who had more than just a bathroom with a view – it didn't even have a door leading into it and faced directly down the staircase. Quite a surprise for any unsuspecting house guest. 'You don't know whether your bathroom's gonna be there in the morning, or whether she's demolished it in the night!' said her poor long-suffering partner. Another intrepid lady in Wales tried to remove an under-stairs cupboard by karate-kicking it. On another occasion we met a lady who, after smashing an entire wall down with just a hammer, had no idea what to do next and promptly gave up.

I particularly remember a young man named Darren, who had received endless abuse for the state of the front room, and not only from his girlfriend, but his girlfriend's grandmother, Rita, too. She was furious at Darren's complete inability to get anything finished as patch-up after patch-up had got him no nearer a finished room – most of our DIY horrors are testosterone induced.

Tools & Materials

You don't need a van load of tools to carry out the basic level of repair and maintenance on your home. If you select your toolkit carefully, and then invest in quality, you can soon build up a modest but flexible combination, easily capable of tackling most everyday DIY duties.

◀ Putting screws into brick or concrete walls is pretty much impossible without the right wallplug. They come in a variety of disguises, but the two main categories are for use in either solid walls or cavity walls (plasterboard).

◀ There are different drill bits designed to make holes in wood, metal and masonry. Get the right type for the right job, and then store them so you always know which is which.

▲ Molegrips are an adjustable sized pair of pliers that will lock into position once closed. Great for holding small objects while they glue, or gripping larger objects when you're trying to pull them apart.

▲ Possibly the most useful powertool you will ever own (see pages 18 and 19).

▲ The most common errors in DIY are caused by inaccurate measurements. Get a decent retractable metal rule that is robust and accurate.

◄ A medium-weight hammer is always useful. Get one with a claw as part of the head and you'll be able to pull out old loose nails as well.

▲ Either invest in a small set of varying sized screwdrivers with both crosshead and slothead ends, or get a system where one handle will accept a whole range of different attachments.

▲ A blunt knife is much more dangerous than a sharp one. Keep your blades in good condition so that they cut without slipping. A knife with retractable replaceable blades is the best option.

◄ When you need to shed a bit of extra light on some gloomy corner of the loft while you work, then a torch is just the thing. If you can't trust yourself to keep fresh batteries available, then get a rechargeable one.

►If you get the right glue for the materials you are bonding, and then follow the manufacturer's instructions as to how it should be applied, you can stick pretty much anything to anything, confident that it will stay there forever.

▲ A proper set of steps will enable you to get into the right position to tackle any of those frustrating high-level jobs, and keep you safe while you're doing them.

◄The human hand has not been designed to do what pliers can do for you. A reasonable sized pair will grip onto whatever you need to twist or pull with far more force than your fingers ever could. Many pliers also have additional features that will let you cut or strip electrical wire.

Getting Started

For the purpose of this book, and from bitter experience on the programme, repairs and improvements can largely be classified in the following way. 'Improvements' are what people do to their houses to either impress or placate their partners and/or children, while 'repairs' are what the *DIY SOS* team have to do once it becomes clear that not only are the partners/children distinctly unimpressed, they also now have nowhere to wash or cook or even eat... The complexity of the repairs is usually a direct result of the scale of the 'improvements', but we are basically talking here about anything from fixing a window to knocking new holes through walls. Whatever the project, there is always one golden rule to bear in mind. It's the one rule that if everyone obeyed, we wouldn't have a programme to make at all: KNOW YOUR LIMITATIONS. It's not complicated, not long-winded and pretty easy to remember – or so you would have thought...

Despite its reputation in certain quarters, DIY is actually a very logical and straightforward process. However, starting things that you don't really know how to finish is not the best way to get into it. Mind you, this does not mean that the extent of your entire DIY career must now be limited to what you are currently qualified to attempt. Far from it. There are endless books out there which will help to get you up to speed on all manner of domestic DIY projects. All we suggest is that you read something relevant before you tackle something new. On the following pages you will find a selection of projects which detail many of the day-to-day chores around the average house. You've probably been called upon to attempt one or two of them already, now you can find out where it all went wrong... Even if you don't actually need to tackle any of these projects right now, why not spend some time flicking through the pages anyway. You may well find that there are tips and techniques featured here that will be just as applicable to some of those other little jobs that we don't specifically mention, but are queuing up in your house even as you hide in your armchair reading this. Tackled professionally and tackled knowledgeably, there are a huge number of DIY tasks that you can complete very satisfactorily around the house. Tasks which will genuinely improve the quality of your time at home, and ultimately increase the value of that home when it's time to move on. So pull up a workbench (use it to put your feet up) and read on...

Step by Step

Choosing A Power Drill

WARNING! Take care with Powertools

CHOOSING A POWER DRILL

Step 1

Always follow the manufacturer's instructions! A drill's power is measured in volts. 12v is a bit limiting, 14v is good for almost any job, 18v or above will go through anything. Go for a cordless version. If it's a money choice, go for a powerful corded drill.

Step 2

The chuck is the bit that you put the attachments into: almost every drill has one with the same maximum size (10mm). Older drills use a chuck key to fix the attachments in place; more modern devices have a simple twist grip which you can do with your hand.

Step 3

Almost every drill will now have a forward and reverse action (vital if you want to use it as a screwdriver as well as a drill), but you should also try to get what's called 'hammer action' as this will allow you to drill into the most stubborn masonry and concrete.

Using A Power Drill

Step 1

Always use the right attachment for the job in hand. Know exactly what you're looking for when you buy drill bits (right) and read the packaging carefully first. Store everything in an orderly fashion so that you still know what's intended to drill what, later on.

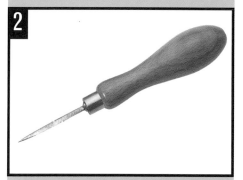

Step 2

Mark your drilling point before you start – a pencil cross is perfectly OK, but a little indentation made with a bradawl is even better. Always know just how deep you need to drill before. Ensure there are no water pipes or cables hidden beneath the surfaces.

Step 3

Drilling slowly, make sure that your hole is appearing where it's supposed to be. Stay straight. Unless you specifically wish to drill a hole at an angle, keep the drill at right angles to the wall as you go in. Always follow the manufacturer's instructions.

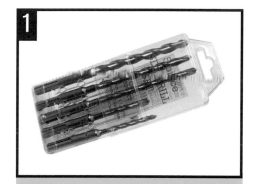

USING A POWER DRILL

Step by Step

Fixing A Curtain Pole

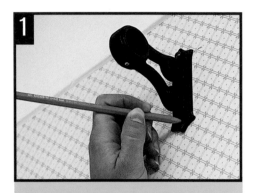

Step 1

Hold the curtain rail in position. Use a spirit level to draw a guideline above the window where you want the brackets to be. Mark through the screw holes of each bracket to establish a fixing point on the wall. Watch out for cables or pipes beneath the surface.

Step 2

If the wall is masonry, drill holes long enough for the fixing to penetrate the structural material, not just the plaster. Fit rawl plugs. (If the wall is hollow, use cavity fixings or cut and screw a timber softwood batten 25mm thick on which to mount the brackets.)

Step 3

Now put the curtain pole into position. Some designs will require you to slide the pole through the brackets before you fix them into place, while others might need all the curtain rings to be threaded into place before you put the pole into its finished position.

FIXING A CURTAIN POLE

Case Study

Caroline & Dave

If you've got a baby on the way the pair of you will have your hands full with kitting the house out with all those essential nursery items. It will also be a priority to have the house in tip-top condition, with everything needing to be kept clean and sterile, particularly the kitchen where the wee sprite's food will be prepared. When we visited Caroline and Dave in their Plymouth home, we found that even though they had already achieved half the equation (Caroline was successfully pregnant!), their kitchen left a lot to be desired.

For nine years the couple have prepared food in a kitchen with no sink, no cupboards and not a scrap of wall plaster to speak of. We had serious work to do, so while Caroline put her feet up, Brigid, our designer, reached for the drawing board and began plotting.

The first thing that had to go was a separating wall. Once this was out of the way, the kitchen was a lot more spacious and airy. With the wall taken down, a reinforced steel joist was inserted, spanning the width of the ceiling to support the extra weight.

A man from the council's planning department had to be contacted so that he could pay us a visit and hopefully approve our efforts as safe. He hated it and so we then had to build

the wall back up again. Only kidding! The support beam was approved and we were able to move on to the next stage of the work.

By this point Dave the Homeowner was earning himself the nickname of Dave The Destroyer, having taken great pleasure in sledgehammering the wall and ripping out whatever else needed to go. He also tried his hand at plastering (the job was made easier by the fact that there was no old plaster to remove from the walls in the first place) and bonded with Chris, our team plasterer, over baby talk.

While they chatted, we worked our socks off. There were a few of those technical and artistic disagreements which really do occur among the team. Billy, our spark, rashly questioned the time Brigid had spent on decorating a door, to which Brigid retorted, 'that's why I'm a designer, and you're an electrician' –

ouch! Arguments aside, by the end everyone was thrilled with the result, door included.

I've got cupboards! I've never had cupboards before!' exclaimed a delighted Caroline. Burnt red walls livened the place up no end to turn Caroline and Dave's dingy, cramped kitchen into a warm, spacious haven, with enough room for a table and chairs to accommodate a thriving family with many children.

Step by Step

Fitting A Mortise Lock

Step 1

It's often easier to unscrew the hinges and remove the door completely when fitting new locks. Hold the new lock in position against the face of the door to mark off its length and draw two lines across the edge with a try square.

Step 2

Take a marking gauge and scribe a central line position between these two lines. Alternatively, measure the centre point from both edges and draw a pencil line with a ruler.

Step 3

Now line up the lock back in position on the door edge and then mark a position for the body of the lock using a try square as before.

FITTING A MORTISE LOCK

Step 4

Apply tape to a flat-ended drill bit to indicate the depth of the lock body. Now drill a series of overlapping holes along the centre line. It is important to keep the drill absolutely vertical as you make these holes so that the lock will fit perfectly into place.

Step 5

Carefully chisel out any waste from the new slot you have created and then slide the lock body home. Mark around the end plate with a craft knife and chisel out a recess so the end plate sits flush in the door.

Step 6

Remove the lock and line it up against the face of the door. Use a bradawl to indicate the position of the new keyhole and the new spindle position. Now drill and clean out the two holes Finally, replace the body of the lock and check that it is working freely. Fit the end cover and handles.

FITTING A MORTISE LOCK

Step by Step

Fixing A Rotten Sill

Step 1

Use a hammer (ideally a mallet) and wood chisel to chop away the rotten sill to create a sound and level base, right back to where the wood is good and solid. Take a little care though as it is important to avoid chiselling into any existing nails or screws.

Step 2

Now take a handsaw (or hire an electric jigsaw) and cut the new wooden sill to length, making a 45-degree angle at each end. Check the sill during this marking and cutting process to test the fit as you go along and adjust it as necessary.

Step 3

Apply a specially designed timber filler/adhesive all along the back of the existing sill and base of the new sill. Using firm pressure, press and bed the sill into position. If the sill requires extra fixing, drill through the front edge and screw it into the old sill.

FIXING A ROTTEN SILL

Step 4

Only when the new sill is securely fixed in position can you measure and cut the shorter side pieces. Measure, cut and fit these in the same way as the longer length. Again, use long screws to secure the new timber in place if the adhesive isn't holding firm.

Step 5

Finally, remove all the excess adhesive from your new sill and fill the screw holes and gaps (if any) as necessary. Leave the adhesive for 24 hours to fully set before lightly sanding off any rough edges. Prime and top coat to finish.

FIXING A ROTTEN SILL

Carol, Michael & Lizzie

Most people tend to use their attic as a storeroom for suitcases, Christmas decorations and cardboard boxes. But if you are a bit more daring and have other places to hoard your junk, you might even want to live in it. Loft conversions can often be a nightmare and making the loft a safe, friendly environment to sleep in is a lot of hard work. We travelled to Herefordshire to meet Carol, Michael and their young daughter Lizzie. Poor little Lizzie was sleeping in a very ugly bedroom, which was cold and draughty, with tiny gaps in the walls letting gusts of cold air in.

Though Carol admits that she enjoys doing a bit of DIY, saying that she needs a few directional tips would be an understatement. Sorry, Carol, but even your husband only gives you 2 out of 10 for technical ability! In converting the room in the first place, Carol had a brainwave to cut some corners and save some cash. Though money-saving schemes are of course always welcome – in fact, *DIY SOS* swears that saving a few bob and using your initiative is the key to a successful home DIY project – sometimes the only thing that will do is the genuine article.

In this instance, instead of using standard insulation, Carol had stuffed dry straw beneath the floorboards to keep the room warm. Though this is fine for stables, straw is highly flammable and is certainly not a desirable option for keeping the kiddies warm. There is also the chance that it could rot and cause structural damage to the rest of the house. In a nutshell, it had to go.

We only had one day to turn the room into a paradise for Lizzie, so we got to work straight away on getting the flooring insulated and fitting a snug carpet to keep little toes toasty. Then it was onto the walls and ceiling. Carol showed her flair for sawing (technical ability 10 out of 10, Michael!) and before long, frames had been mounted against the walls and new wooden interiors were fitted. Doing

this may limit the room by a couple of inches, but separating the exterior wall with a new interior surface cuts out the draught and removes the cold edge of an outside wall.

With the room now draught proof, it was painted in a series of lovely warm colours and sections of wallpaper were used as a frieze that stretched right round the room and co-ordinated with the curtains and bedspread. This also gave extra depth to the attic, as horizontal lines create the illusion that the room is longer than it actually is. Carol gave us a hand by making her daughter a toy box so that the room didn't end up looking too cluttered and cramped, and then we were finished.

Happily, Lizzie loved her new room.

Step by Step

Repairing A Sash Window

Step 1

For serious DIYers only! Take hold of the remaining sash cord and cut through it with a sharp knife, lower the weights and release. Prise off the staff beads that hold the window in place. Now you may remove the window from the frame.

Step 2

Remove old nails and cords from the surround and rub wax on the sides. Carefully prise out the two parting beads from their grooves to reveal the two lower-weight pockets at the bottom of the frame. Lift these out and remove both weights and old cords.

Step 3

Clean up and oil the pulley wheels at the top of the frame and tie a 'mouse' (any small weight) to a length of thin string and drop it through the hole above the pulley wheel. Feed it down and out of the lower-weight pocket.

REPAIRING A SASH WINDOW

Step 4

Tie the string to the new sash cord and draw it through the top and out of the pocket as before. Use a double knot to retie the old weight to the new cord, and repeat this whole process on the other side of the frame.

Step 5

Pull the weight to the top of the pulleys and wind it around a screwdriver so the weight is in position and the cord dangles free. Now hold the window on the bottom ledge, pull the cord into the groove and use clout nails to secure. Don't nail to the very top.

Step 6

Having replaced both the cords, place the window back in the frame to check that it can slide up and down all the way. Refit the pocket hole covers and tap in the lengths of parting bead. Refit the outer staff beads and check the window is running smoothly.

REPAIRING A SASH WINDOW

Step by Step

Plasterboarding A Brick Wall

Step 1

First of all chisel away to remove any excess mortar from the face of the wall, then brush down and prime with PVA sealant to aid adhesion and also to prevent the adhesive from drying out too quickly.

Step 2

Now mix up the dry wall adhesive with clean water in a bucket until a thick paste of whipped cream consistency is formed. (Some drills have an attachment to mix adhesive.)

Step 3

Use chalk to outline the plasterboard sheet size on the wall. Take a trowel and scoop up the adhesive, then use a short punching action to knock the trowel edge against the wall, thus releasing the mix.

PLASTERBOARDING WALLS

Step 4

Continue applying adhesive around the marked outline, then fill in the centre area. Aim to release a similar amount of adhesive with each strike of the trowel (dotting and dabbing), working quickly and evenly down the wall.

Step 5

Line up the plasterboard in position, then press firmly onto your dots and dabs. Take a solid length of timber and perform a short stamping action to bed the board securely in place.

Step 6

Continue working across the wall, staggering each board as you go along. This avoids creating any long horizontal joint lines that might encourage surface cracks to appear once you have decorated. Finally, apply tape to seal gaps in the plasterboard, and filler to make good any cracks or joints, and then sand smooth.

PLASTERBOARDING WALLS

Step by Step

Plasterboarding A Curved Recess

Step 1

Remove any raised mortar and loose material from the brickwork then prime the entire area with PVA (general-purpose liquid adhesive). Carefully measure the width and length of the arch, but aim to cut the plasterboard longer than needed to allow for the trimming.

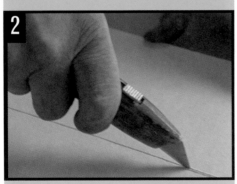

Step 2

Use a straight edge and pencil to mark off the cutting line. Working on a firm base, take a heavy craft knife and score a deep line along the board. For small cuts and trimming, simply snap the board over your knee but for full-size boards, support the whole length.

Step 3

Cut the plasterboard length off and then wet both sides of the board with water. Place the board against a wall, curving out the bottom as much as it will allow without it breaking, then leave it in place overnight.

PLASTERBOARDING CURVES

Step 4

Place the board into position and trim to length. Mix up some dry lining adhesive and thickly spread it over the back of the board. Now, starting at the top of the arch, press the board up against the brickwork and then bed it into position.

Step 5

Get someone to help you by holding the board while you knock in a few plasterboard or masonry nails to secure it into place. Finally, remove any excess adhesive.

Step 6

If necessary, fit a sheet of plasterboard (dry lining) to the rest of the area and then finish off with a skim coat of plaster. When the damp patches have dried out, leave everything for one complete week before decorating.

PLASTERBOARDING CURVES

Step by Step

Making a Door in a Lath and Plaster Wall

Step 1

Make sure the wall isn't load bearing or protected under planning preservation laws. Old walls can produce dust on removal, so wet the floor first and wear a dust mask. Knock off the plaster and pull away the laths from the vertical studs.

Step 2

Saw through and remove the vertical timber studs. Extract any remaining nails and knock off any loose plaster until you have a sound and secure surround for your new opening.

Step 3

Use planed and finished softwood timber to construct a new frame around the inside of the wall opening. Screw through into the existing studs to secure the frame into place.

MAKING A DOOR

Step 4

Infill any remaining large gaps with off-cuts of plasterboard simply nailed into place and then dust off the entire construction. Then prime all over with PVA solution.

Step 5

Neatly make good all the damaged plasterwork right up to the edge of the new opening. A 'one-coat' plaster mix is ideal for this job. Trowel into place with a plasterer's float (see right) for a perfect finish.

Step 6

When all the new plasterwork is fully dry, cut and fit a new timber architrave around the top and two sides. Make good the skirting to meet it at the bottom. Either create your new wall opening to fit a standard sized door, or have your own design made to fit.

MAKING A DOOR

Top Tips

Drilling Holes In Walls

When drilling holes in walls, use masking tape to fix an open plastic bag just beneath the hole to catch the dust.

Drilling To A Certain Depth

Measure the screw against the drill bit and put some masking tape on the drill bit at the appropriate length. Then drill until you reach the edge of the masking tape.

Adhesive Problems

If you are having difficulty in sticking things down, try using silicone bath sealant. It will stick to almost anything, it's waterproof and can be used on porous surfaces, indoors or out. It's the most useful thing in my toolkit.

Smooth Silicon

For a really neat finish when using silicon, first apply the sealant as usual (don't worry about any uneven bits), then spray the silicon bead and surrounding area with water from a plant sprayer. Run a wet finger over the silicon bead to smooth. The silicon will not stick to the wet areas, thus giving a smooth and even filled joint.

Smooth Plaster

Don't be tempted to play around with the plaster, getting it smooth. Doing this will draw the moisture to the surface of the plaster, and it will be a lot more difficult to work with. Wait until the plaster reaches the stage where you can smooth the surface with a steel float without removing the plaster. Reaching this stage will depend on the temperature of the room and the surface of the walls.

Share your views with DIY friends on our website!

Plumbing

Take it from me, there are two people you really don't want knocking at your door in the early hours of the morning: bailiffs and plumbers. Both mean that you have a major problem with your liquidity, and both will probably cost you an arm and a leg to get rid of. Fortunately, one of these is a very unlikely scenario, for as we all know you can never get a plumber to knock on your door any time before lunch at the earliest. The water system in your house is one of those things that everyone thinks is far too complicated to get involved with at a DIY level and is definitely best left to 'a man who knows'. And while you can cause yourself some major problems if you do try to tackle major plumbing problems without a thorough knowledge of what you're doing, those situations are the exception rather than the rule. Contrary to what the plumber may tell you, moving hot and cold water around your house is not that complex a process. Understand the basics and you're well on the way to becoming a pretty competent player in the watersports arena. Among the many benefits to becoming qualified in this way is that you'll find yourself reaching for a spanner instead of a phone the next time the tap starts dripping...

'Why get wet?' asks Lowri.

'"We always do girlie rooms," he said."Why don't we do a boy's room for a change?" Bob put his tools down, but Brigid put her foot down, and the en-suite bedroom it was.'

If your only plumbing dabble to date is cleaning the bath out every couple of days then read on, and be prepared for a timely lesson or two. Of all the rooms in the house that can cause nightmares, the bathroom seems to be there right at the top of the list. On our travels we are forever encountering seemingly insurmountable problems with the pipework, but the *DIY SOS* building team assure me that you don't have to be the plumbing equivalent of Stephen Hawking to put things right. There is now a range of 'push fit' fittings in the shops that completely does away with bending copper pipes and messing around with solder and blow torches.

In fact, nowadays, plumbing is actually one of those jobs that isn't really all that bad once you get into it, though unlike other DIY tasks (such as sawing a kitchen unit to size, where any mistake will simply leave you with less work surface), a serious error in the plumbing department may well result in the shower no longer being restricted just to the bathroom, but regularly shared out to every other room in the house as well. Still, they say cleanliness is next to godliness.

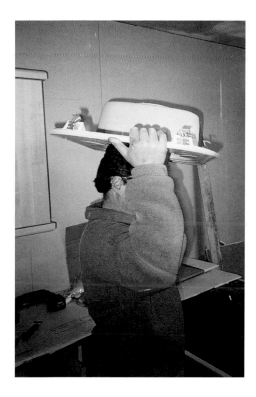

Chris the plasterer. His golden rule is to always measure twice, cut once and only mix enough material to complete the job you are doing.

If all that hasn't put you off – and I hope it hasn't, then let's think positive and revel in a few of our own *DIY SOS* plumbing triumphs. Do you remember when we visited a couple named Roland and Catherine in their Southend home, ultimately turning a bedroom and connecting cupboard into a very fancy en-suite affair? It was a job that Bob originally didn't want to tackle, being a toss-up between that and the games room downstairs. 'We always do girlie rooms,' he said. 'Why don't we do a boy's room for a change?' Although Bob put his tools down, Brigid decided to put her foot down, and the en-suite bedroom it

was. Our devious little designer had even managed to sketch out plans for the bedroom in advance, and clearly never had any intention at all of being lured downstairs to the games room in the first place.

The Southend project turned into much more than a simple renovation task. We actually built a bathroom from scratch, fitting an entire suite with all new inlet and outlet piping, and connecting the new toilet to the existing sewers, which meant contacting the authorities first. Are you scared yet, or just inspired?

And do you remember meeting a couple called Mark and Fiona? They were having some trouble getting a fresh drink of water. Mark had cleverly connected the taps so that they all ran with hot water and the only way to get a drop of cold was to turn the tap on so hard that the water whizzed through the boiler far too quickly to become heated. Sounds hygenic, doesn't it? I can assure you there was more than a drink of water to celebrate when we sorted that one out.

Tools & Materials

You aren't going to need anything complex in your toolkit to tackle basic plumbing problems. There are a couple of specialist tools you might want to invest in, but for most jobs you may well have all you need already. Clean and dry your tools after the last job, and they'll still be ready and working for the next one.

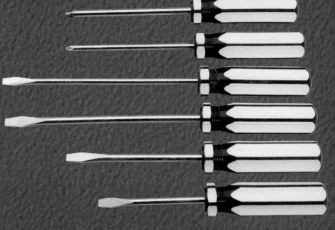

◀ **Molegrips** are an adjustable sized pair of pliers that will lock into position once closed. Great for holding small objects while they glue, or gripping larger objects when you're trying to pull them apart.

▲ Either invest in a small set of varying sized screwdrivers with both crosshead and slothead ends, or get a system where one handle will accept a whole range of different types of attachments.

◀ Using a hacksaw to cut pipes can be very inaccurate and frustrating. A pipecutter is by far the best way to tackle the job. Make sure you get one that has the capacity to handle whichever sized pipe you are working with.

◄ This is a short bladed saw designed to cut through metal, which is hard, so don't expect to make much progress very quickly. Hacksaws need to be used with a lot of patience. They take replaceable blades, so always make sure you have a sharp one to hand.

◄ Blocked sinks or baths often just need a quick plunger attack to free them up. Pumping the plunger over the plughole forces pressure down the pipe to clear the obstruction. Always remember to cover the overflow hole first before you start.

▲ Strong gloves (and a strong stomach) are a must when working with blocked wastepipes. It goes without saying that they need to be waterproof as well.

▲ A good adjustable spanner is a must, as just about every nut or retaining ring you come across is going to be a different size to the last one. If you grow to like plumbing (and some people do) you might want to invest in small set of adjustable spanners to cover all eventualities.

▲ A floorboard saw has teeth right around the nose and is specially designed so that you can cut and lift just part of a fitted floorboard to get at the problem underneath.

Getting Started

OK, pay attention at the back, this is what you've been waiting for. Everything you need to know about a domestic water supply in under three minutes... Well, nearly everything. Here comes the science...

Essentially every house is plumbed in the same way. From the high pressure 'mains' (usually under the pavement or street) you get what's called a 'rising main' coming into your property. Somewhere in your house (often hidden under the kitchen sink, or possibly in the cellar if you have one) is the 'main stopcock' which can turn this supply on and off. One of the first things you need to do before tackling any plumbing problem is to locate that 'main stopcock' and make sure it works. If you can't stop the water coming into your house you have precious little chance of fixing any problems it creates further down the line. Your side of the stopcock, this rising main usually goes straight up into the loft and fills a large cold water storage tank, or 'cistern', which lives up there. The cold water cistern is right at the top of your house for one good reason – from here on in, all the water that runs around the hot and cold taps of your house is delivered there by gravity, and the higher your cold water cistern the more efficient that system of delivery is going to be. Cold water runs straight from the cistern, hot water sits in a heating cylinder first, but both use gravity to arrive at the taps. The hot water cylinder may also be up in the loft, but is more likely to be a floor below in an airing cupboard or something similar.

Alongside, but completely separate to this system, the central heating water is electrically pumped in a continuous circuit through the boiler, to all the radiators and then back to the boiler again to reheat. The central heating system is not a completely closed loop. Up in your loft you will probably have a little mains fed 'header tank' (with another floating valve and overflow pipe system) that keeps the central heating water topped up as it evaporates, which it does all the time.

That's it. Anything you do to the plumbing system in your house, or anything it does to you, will be connected to one of these two systems. Some people may have a completely different type of central heating, but everyone will have a hot and cold tap water system which works along these lines. Don't be intimidated by the plumbing any longer. There are always things you can be doing to make it work better for you, and on the following pages are a few key projects to get you going...

Step by Step

Clearing Blocked Sinks

CLEARING BLOCKED SINKS

Step 1

If a sink is slow to empty there is likely to be a build up of grease and debris, usually in the trap or waste pipes. Try to clear it initially with a proprietary chemical cleaner. Always follow all the instructions supplied carefully. If that proves unsuccessful, the 'Classic' sink plunger may be employed. Smear the rim of the rubber cup with petroleum jelly and place it over the plughole. Fill the sink a quarter of the way up, hold a wet cloth over the overflow hole and pump the handle up and down until the water drains away.

Step 2

Another method for clearing a blocked sink is to use a hand-operated water pump. First, block the sink overflow with a damp cloth. Fill the pump with water and hold this into the plughole. Start pumping using a firm up and down motion. The downward pump forces a powerful jet of water into the trap and along the pipe, while the upward stroke creates suction.

Step 3

A third method is the sink auger, which is a flexible clearing rod. This method may be more suitable if the trap underneath the sink is an old design (possibly metal) and less accessible than a plastic one (see step 4). Simply push the rod down into the trap and crank the handle in both directions to dislodge the blockage.

Step 4

If the above prove unsuccessful then remove the access cap on the base of your sink trap. If this is not possible then the whole trap will need to be removed. Start by making sure the sink plug is in and place a bucket under the trap. Plastic traps are designed to be only handtight, so removal for cleaning will be fairly straightforward.

CLEARING BLOCKED SINKS

Step by Step

Repairing A Burst Pipe

Step 1

A burst pipe can be temporarily repaired with an epoxy putty repair kit. For a long-term repair, you will need to cut out the damaged part of the pipe, if it's obvious, and replace it. For a quick solution use an off-cut of garden hose. Split the hose lengthways and slide it over the damaged area, then bind it with 3 or 4 jubilee clips.

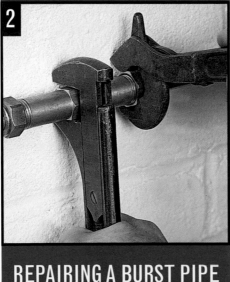

Step 2

Alternatively you could use a compression nut 'slip coupling' to replace the damaged section of pipe. Pull back the coupling to connect with the other cut end. Unscrew the compression nuts and slide them together with the olives (metal rings) along the pipe so they are clear of the screw threads. Apply PTFE (Polytetrafluorethylene) sealing tape clockwise around the exposed screw threads and slide the olives and nuts back. Hand tighten in position. Finally, tighten the compression joints by using two spanners.

REPAIRING A BURST PIPE

Russell & Claire

As far as botch job bathrooms go, this one was the weirdest you are ever likely to see. It belongs to Russell and Claire and suffered from very porous walls, with swirling great hunks of filler lumped everywhere. It looked as if filler was actually growing from various parts of the bathroom in organic-looking tendril chunks, sometimes pointing out more than an inch, leering and watching as you used the facilities. The sorry state of the chip-prone walls had made Russell reach for the quick-fire patch-up kit too often. Though what this bathroom really needed wasn't speedy DIY, it was some TLC. The first thing we did was to throw Russell's filler gun away, then made some inspections of the walls he had gunned. Luckily, much of his efforts were not in vain and after the walls were sanded and the filler was tidied up, Russell had in fact saved us some time. A layer of mistcoat was added (a solution 50% water, 50% emulsion). This helped to show up any pits and grooves the brittle wall was hiding, so that we could go back and smooth them out, before adding the final layers. The rotten tongue-and-groove wood was removed from behind the shower and in its place we used aquaboard (a waterproof alternative to plyboard). The shower area was tiled to keep things watertight, and we stuck a unique tile, made by Tom, Russell and Claire's little boy, above the sink.

Russell said he wanted some shelves hung from the tiled wall, which meant drilling holes directly into the tiles – a task not as daring as it seems if you remember to cheat: place a piece of masking tape on the appropriate tile and drill through that. This prevents chipping and absorbs all the nasty vibrations that cause cracks.

We decided to use a sealant strip along the edge of the bath adjacent to the wall to stop any water from running

down the gap and causing unseen damage. Most households tend to use a silicone sealant for this, gunned along the area where the bath and wall tiles meet. Using silicone sealant is not wrong, but it never lasts very long because when a person gets into a full bath, the bath lowers slightly, tearing the sealant. So fill the bath up as high as you can with water, apply the sealant, and then a couple of hours later, let the water out. The result will be a fully sealed bath.

And that was that. We painted the bathroom walls tangerine to warm the place up a bit and everyone was happy.

Step by Step

Bleeding A Radiator

Step 1

One of the simplest maintenance routines for central heating is venting or 'bleeding' the radiators. If a radiator is hot at the bottom and cool at the top, it probably contains trapped air. If the system is noisy (the sound of 'rushing water' in the pipes), this may also be cured by bleeding the radiators.

Step 2

Turn off the heating and place an old rag along the base of the radiator. Hold another rag around the edge of the panel just below the venting point. Put a radiator key in the air vent and turn it slowly anticlockwise until it hisses. Wait until the water starts to come through, then quickly close the vent.

Step 3

When the water is released from the vent it has a tendency to splatter and it is often dirty, which may possibly cause staining to the surrounding decoration. To avoid this, a number of bleed key attachments are available to direct the water safely away.

BLEEDING A RADIATOR

Step by Step

Fitting A Radiator Thermostatic Valve

Step 1

First turn off both valves. Drain down the radiator (rad) into a bowl by loosening the main nut between the radiator and the valve (see step 2). Open the air vent at the top of the radiator to assist the flow. Fully undo both nuts and remove the old valve.

Step 2

Wind PTFE tape tightly around all the threads four times and assemble back onto the connections. Hand-tighten the nuts before using two wrenches as before. The photo demonstrates a radiator tail also being taped (only necessary to fit to a new radiator).

Step 3

Finally, fit the thermostatic valve top and then refill the radiator to bleed and test for leaks. To eliminate small leaks, only a slight turn is normally required. NOTE: Always use two wrenches when working on valves to counteract the twisting pressure on the copper pipe. If unsure, consult a professional.

FITTING A RAD VALVE

Step by Step

Hanging A New Radiator

Step 1

First, mark the central position of the brackets on the top of the radiator with a pencil.

Step 2

Position the radiator up against the wall, check that it's level, then draw a horizontal and vertical line at the bracket points previously marked. Before you start drilling ensure there are no pipes or cables beneath the surface.

Step 3

Now line one wall bracket up with the lines you have drawn. Mark through the bracket slots and then drill the holes ready for fixing. (It may be necessary to change the line of height to suit various types of skirting board.)

HANGING A NEW RADIATOR

Step 4

Using suitable wall plugs and screws, and depending on the type of wall and radiator size, screw one bracket to the wall. Now fit the second bracket, checking with a level across the two before finally securing it into place.

Step 5

Ideally two people should now lift the radiator onto the brackets from each end. Should this not be possible, try making a shoulder strap to ease the job along.

Step 6

If you need to fit tails to the radiator ends, working back towards the nut, tightly wind PTFE tape around the tail threads (approximately five times). This must then be fully tightened in with the appropriate key.

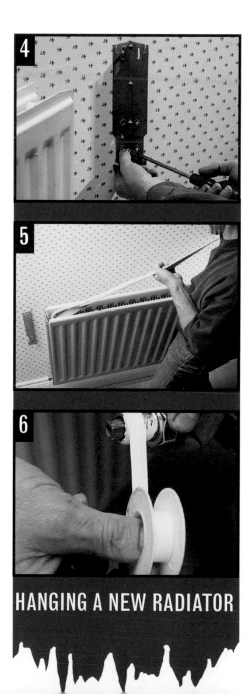

HANGING A NEW RADIATOR

Step by Step

Installing A Washing Machine Waste Outlet

INSTALLING A WASTE PIPE

Step 1

The standard method of running a washing machine outlet hose usually employs a vertical plastic standpipe, attached to a trap to avoid the possibility of the waste water being siphoned back into the machine. The machine hose fits loosely into the open-ended pipe. If an existing waste pipe runs behind the intended machine position, then a non-return valve kit can be purchased and easily fitted into the line. Check first that there is a trap in the run. If not, you must fit one.

Step 2

All the materials you need to carry out this project can be purchased as a standard kit from most DIY stores. Unscrew the 'saddle' from the rest of the drain kit and place it around the existing waste pipe. Screw it down and secure it in position.

Step 3

Now screw the cutting tool supplied into the saddle bracket. This should be done until a hole has been cut into the waste pipe. Remove the tool and screw on the rest of the drain kit. If in doubt read the manufacturer's instructions.

Step 4

The standpipe can either be a long (as shown) or short connector. However, both will contain a non-return valve to prevent any water flowing back into the machine. Finally, push the machine outlet hose over the coupling and then secure with a hose clip. The machine is now ready to use.

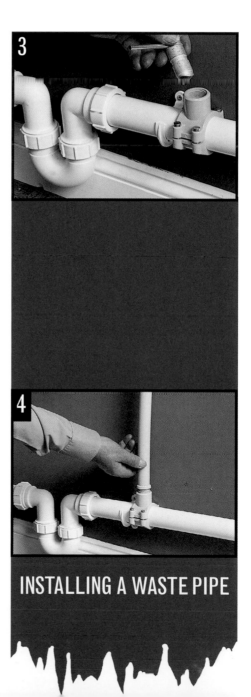

INSTALLING A WASTE PIPE

Roland & Catherine

Here's a tip for you: If you are moving into a house that 'needs a bit of work' and your partner says it's the perfect opportunity to try and cut some costs by doing all the repairs yourself, then beware. Make sure your partner is really ready to take on the job of decorating, especially if their DIY track record stops short at assembling a catalogue coffee table.

Roland and Catherine moved into a spacious abode in Southend with the intent to do it up royally, but a year down the line they were still living, eating and sleeping in a nightmare. Roland once made a start on the electric wiring, but after a certain amount of play with green, yellow and blue wires, decided to stop. Why? Because he's colour blind. Yikes! Come forth *DIY SOS*!

There was a little bit of double-dealing at play when we visited Roland and Catherine. Catherine went off for a few days, thinking we were just there to do the games room, but we had other ideas. Builder Bob organised a small group of people to spend some time on colouring and furnishing the games room, while upstairs everyone else was full steam ahead on turning a shabby bedroom and closet into an en-suite dream.

This meant a lot of work – trust me, building a bathroom from scratch is one of the hardest things you can ever take on, and especially if you plan to do it all in just a couple of days. There's plumbing as well as positioning, and only the most daring DIY enthusiast should attempt to try it.

We had to employ a military-like precision to co-ordinate everybody so that not a minute was wasted –

though hopefully, your DIY can be stretched out over a more relaxed period. We had people steaming the wallpaper off, we had people chalking out where to position the bathroom suite, and we had Brigid falling out with Bob over Feng Shui, for a change.

I don't think we have ever been so close to the edge of a deadline before – especially with the plumbing, which is a job you certainly don't want to rush unless you are planning to fit showers in more rooms than just the bathroom. But thankfully, everything upstairs fell neatly into place.

Catherine was pretty unimpressed when she returned and first saw the games room, which we had painted a deep blue, filled with entertainment, but had not even bothered adding a skirting board to! Then we took her upstairs and she was thrilled.

She loved the folding screens we added to separate the bedroom from the en-suite facilities. These were standard MDF boards that you can buy from any DIY store. We painted and hinged them, and along with Brigid's mix of painted ceramic and cork tiles, they created a romantic look.

Now they had a royal abode.

TopTips

Bath Sealant

When applying sealant around the edge of lightweight baths, make sure the bath is full of water so that the sealant doesn't tear when full.

Cutting Tiles

Mark the line on the tile first of all. Using a tile guillotine, nibble away at the edge of the tile, working your way towards the line, taking away a little at a time. Do not try to cut straight down the line because the tile will shatter.

Drilling Tiles

When drilling through wall tiles, place a piece of masking tape over the tile and drill through the tape. If you're using an electric drill, I'd suggest a slow speed to start. The tape helps prevent the drill bit 'skidding' and the glaze on the tile cracking.

Removing Tile Cement

After chiselling off old ceramic tiles, you can remove any leftover tile adhesive with a steam wallpaper stripper and a filling knife. The steam softens the adhesive, allowing you to scrape it away. Care is needed to avoid gouging the plaster and don't try it on unplastered plasterboard stud partitions. After doing this and a bit of filling, I've been able to paint the wall with emulsion.

Removing Tile Cement

If you've removed ceramic tiles from a plasterboard wall, here's an easy way to remove any tile cement without gouging the plasterboard. Fill a spray bottle with lukewarm water and a couple of drops of washing-up liquid, then spray this onto the tile cement and leave for about ten minutes. Now you can scrape off the tile cement. If there are any stubborn bits, simply repeat the spraying and scraping – you'll be left with a nice clean wall.

Share your views with DIY friends on our website!

Electrics

All through the floors and the walls and the ceilings of your house there is an invisible network of wires and junction boxes that provide light, power and sometimes heat to the rooms around you. However, even though the mechanics of its inner workings lie hidden within the fabric of the buildings it serves, electricity (unlike plumbing) is one of those things that everyone seems to be dangerously comfortable with.

Yet electricity needs to be treated with respect and not played with. The only reason it is not responsible for more DIY accidents is that a huge amount of technology and ingenuity goes into making it as safe as possible. Every electrical appliance you own should have a fuse inside it, designed to cut the power if something goes wrong. Every electrical circuit in your house has more fuses, should that system fail. Once you understand that all these safety procedures are working, there are any number of repairs and improvements you can make to the electrical fittings and fixtures in your house. In this next section of the book we take you through the basics of those procedures, hopefully inspiring you on to bigger and brighter projects.

'Strike a light,' says Lowri.

'Sadly, not everyone has access to Billy. They're left to their own efforts, which can be pretty hopeless... But it really is something you should try.'

Now, this is not a subject for the faint-hearted or the easily distracted as a botched electrical job could well leave you in the dark – emotionally, physically and quite possibly, even permanently. If you are in any doubt, seek professional help with all things electrical. We once met a lady who lost her temper with her kitchen lighting. She hit it with a broom handle and the family was subsequently forced to eat by candlelight every night. It sounds romantic until you realise that all the food preparation was illuminated by a single table lamp plugged into wall sockets wherever she needed to work. By the time we arrived, she told me that carrying a light around with her all over the kitchen was now second nature. Luckily, we managed to shed some permanent light on the kitchen in just one day and then redecorated it so that she also had something good to look at.

Mostly, it's just about getting the right coloured wires in the right places, and so long as you're not colour blind everything should be fine. Unlike one individual we met, who was colour blind and had ripped out most of the light switches from the walls of his

**Billy, AKA The Prince
of Darkness. His golden rule
is always kill the power
before you start.**

home and then given up the whole job because he couldn't work out how to put anything back!

Luckily, in all our electrical tasks we have a secret weapon – Billy. Although he may be known to us as the Prince of Darkness, he has never let us down on a job yet, despite some of the cowboy workmanship he has had to contend with (and we're not just talking about the rest of the team).

Sadly, not everyone has access to Billy. They are left to their own efforts, which can be pretty hopeless. There is a law these days that means all new electrical appliances have to come already fitted with a plug. Changing one is something that many people never even attempt to do now, but it really is something that you should at least try your hand at. Who knows, the day may come when you spot that 'must-have' old electrical appliance in the junk shop, only to find it doesn't have a plug or the fuse has gone. A rudimentary understanding of the principles of electrics could well mean the difference between that appliance becoming a joy to use, or an ornament.

Electrics is not all screwdrivers and fuseboxes though there is also great

pleasure to be had in planning where to place your lighting in a room. Not everywhere has to be coloured just by paint or wallpaper you know – a little splash of light here and there can add a whole new atmosphere to that tired old bedroom or that drab dining room. In fact, I remember when we lit up a whole fire station rest room for a 'bit of a do'. A lot of spotlighting was used to create indoors what ended up looking like a beautiful starry night.

Get to know the basics of how electricity works and you'll soon find you can dramatically change your surroundings at the flick of a switch.

Tools & Materials

Electricity is a bad thing to fool with if you don't know what you are doing. The right tools for the right job are crucial. Before you try to fix or install anything electrical, switch the power off at the main switch first. Also make sure you read any manufacturer's instructions before you start; they are there for a reason – to keep you alive and healthy.

▶ The human hand has not been designed to do what pliers can do for you. A reasonable sized pair will grip onto whatever you need to twist or pull with far more force than your fingers ever could. Many pliers also have additional features that will let you cut or strip electrical wire.

◀ All electrical wire is covered in a plastic insulation sleeve, colour-coded so that you know what's what. To remove this sleeve when you want to make a connection, use wire strippers. Get ones that cater for a variety of cable sizes.

▶ This one is vital. The electrician's screwdriver is designed to light up when it touches live wire. An insulated handle allows you to use this feature to test for live power before you start work. Some designs allow you to check replacement fuses are working as well.

▲ A blunt knife is more dangerous than a sharp one. Keep your blades in good condition so that they cut without slipping. The best one is a knife with retractable replaceable blades.

▲ Either invest in a small set of varying sized screwdrivers with both crosshead and slothead ends, or get a system where one handle will accept a whole range of different attachments.

▲ A floorboard saw has teeth right around the nose and is specially designed so that you can cut and lift just part of a fitted floorboard out to get at the problem underneath.

◄ If you need to shed a bit of extra light on some gloomy corner of the loft while you work, then a torch is just the thing. If you can't trust yourself to keep fresh batteries available, then get a rechargeable one.

Getting Started

Before we indulge in any kind of discussion as to which projects you can tackle in the world of electricity, let's make sure nothing will go wrong when you do. Electricity runs around your house in a series of loops. Power comes out from the mains down the 'live' wire (usually red) and goes back again down the 'neutral' wire (usually blue). If there is a gap in the loop, the electricity stops. When you put something into that gap – a kettle, for example – or a light bulb, the electricity starts flowing again. To make it easier and safer to place things into these 'gaps' we have a system of plugs, wall sockets and switches. But just because there are no appliances in a particular gap, electricity will not stop trying to complete its loop; it never stops trying. All the time the power is on, the electricity in the live wires is looking for something to jump onto. Water is a particular favourite and if you check your biology books you'll find that we are mostly made out of water. With that in mind, let's run through some basic and fairly universal rules of electrical safety.

If you are working on anything which can be unplugged, then unplug it first. When working on the lighting or wall socket circuits in your house, turn them off at the main fuse box. If your fusebox is well labelled, you should be able to tell which fuse relates to which circuit and only disable the one on which you are working. But if it isn't, then take out each fuse one by one (or throw each switch if supplied) and establish what doesn't work. Label the fuse box properly so that you know what to disable next time. You will usually find that each lighting circuit and each wall socket circuit (or 'ring main') on each floor has a fuse or trip switch of its own. However, there are no set rules so you'll have to experiment to see how your house is wired. Once you have completed any electrical project that involves altering the wiring, check and recheck your work long before you connect it up to the power.

Finally, invest in a mains testing screwdriver. This simple little tool will not only allow you to test for electrical current when the power is live. If you get the right type, it will also let you test whether replacement fuses are working before you put them in. These fuses are the most common cause of an electrical appliance failing and they blow when there is too much power going through them, or the appliance they are protecting has developed a fault. Make sure you work out what the problem is (and then rectify it) before you plug in again with a new fuse in place.

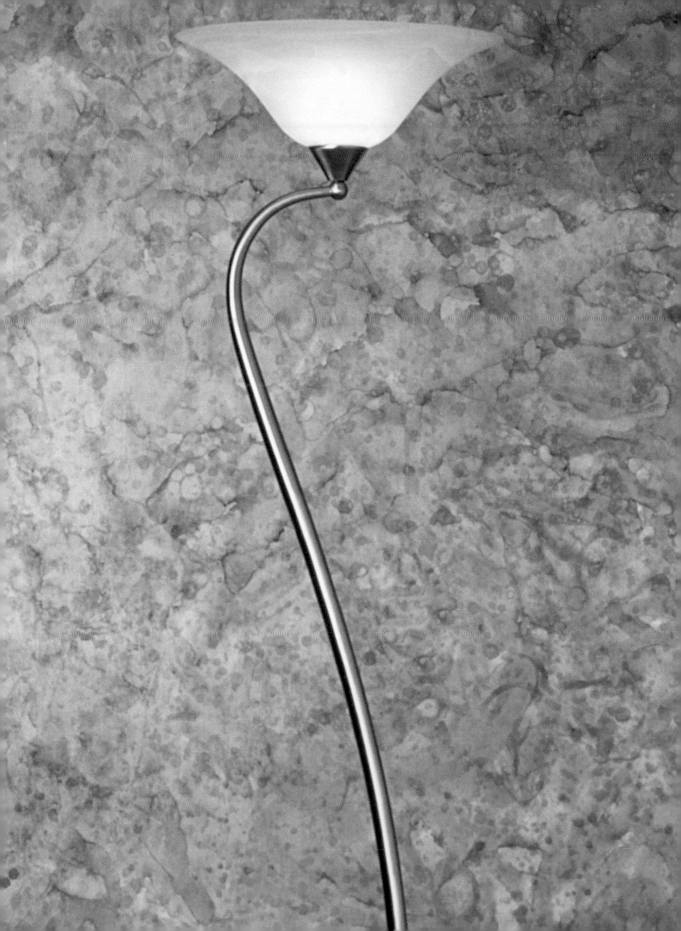

Step by Step

Wiring A Plug

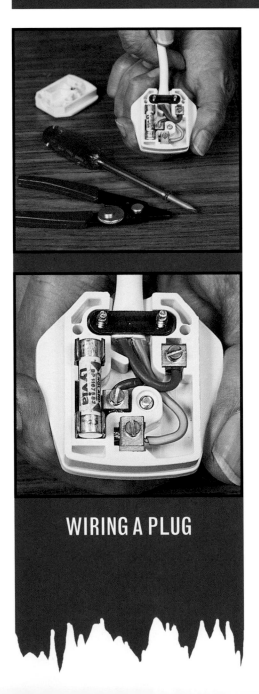

WIRING A PLUG

Step 1

Using the opened plug as a guide, take a sharp knife and trim back the outer cable sheath to the correct length. Note that all plugs will clamp the whole flex at the neck.

Step 2

Now neatly trim back each of the three individual wires so that they fit into the terminals, blue to (N) green and yellow to (E) and brown to (L), avoiding any signs of the bared wire.

Step 3

Twist and fold the bared wire before inserting it into each terminal hole to secure. For clamp type terminals, wind the wire clockwise around the posts and then tighten firmly down. Finally, replace the fuse and then screw the cover back together again. Do not plug in until the plug is re-assembled and the cover has been replaced.
Note: If colours vary, seek advice.

Step by Step

Changing A Fuse

Step 1

New consumer units are fitted with miniature circuit breakers (MCBs). A switch or the push of a button will simply restore power to the broken circuit. Older types require replacing fuse wire or a fuse cartridge.

Step 2

Turn off the main switch and draw out the fuse carrier. Loosen the two fixing screws and remove any old wire. Using wire of the correct amp rating, wind it clockwise around one screw and then tighten. Now pass the wire through and repeat with second screw. Replace the carrier and test.

Step 3

To replace a fuse cartridge, turn off the main switch and draw out the cartridge carrier. Remove the retaining screw and replace with a new cartridge of the same amp rating. Return the carrier and test the circuit.

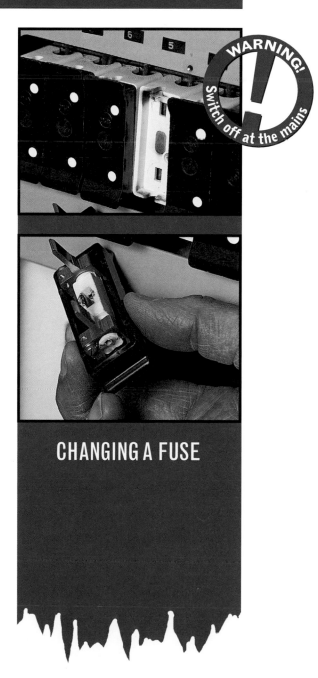

WARNING! Switch off at the mains

CHANGING A FUSE

Step by Step

Changing A Plug Socket

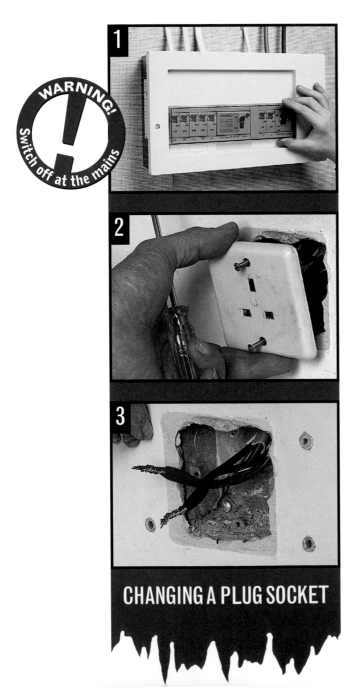

WARNING! Switch off at the mains

CHANGING A PLUG SOCKET

Step 1

First turn off the main switch at the consumer box and remove or switch off the relevant fuse as marked. It is important to always check the socket (single or double) is dead – this can be done with an appliance you know to be working.

Step 2

Using an electricians screwdriver, undo the two screws holding the face plate and gently ease the socket away from the wall. Now loosen the three terminal screws to release the wires from the socket. Check for signs of damage. If in doubt consult an electrician.

Step 3

Now make a note of which wires are connected to each terminal. This will remain the same for your new socket.

Step 4

If there is enough slack from the existing wires, a surface box can be fitted. Simply position the new box centrally over the existing hole and mark through for wall fixings. Note where the cables run in the wall as care must be taken when drilling.

Step 5

Pass the cables through the hole in the new box and then screw into place. Now connect up the double socket as previously noted in step 3. Slide a green-and-yellow earth sleeve over any bare earth wires.

Step 6

Check each group of wires are secure and not trapped before screwing the socket fully into the mounting box. The final picture shows a flush socket. This would require the fitting of a new metal wall box if this is the type of socket you require.

CHANGING A PLUG SOCKET

Graham, Jane & Bridie

Graham was experiencing exactly the same problems every DIY devotee goes through when we visited him and his wife, Jane, in their Devonshire home. He had already completed a few projects on his own, though the fruits of his labours did not always end up exactly as he had planned. Graham had made good sturdy doors that were sadly ill-fitting and wonky, as well as other projects that were almost there, but somehow not quite right.

Jane said she wanted a kitchen that people would visit and instantly be impressed by, so we went to work at turning it into the ultimate culinary environment. Though we never thought we would have this many problems...

First off, there was a solid concrete interior wall that had to be removed. In these cases you may well be tempted to reach for the sledgehammer straight off, but if you have patience and chip through the wall more delicately, progress will be much safer. We wouldn't have know that the wall was full of electrical wires, had Bob just taken to smashing into it and if those wires happened to be live, then you could run the risk of seriously hurting yourself.

Once the wall was down then we thought we were over the worst of it. How wrong could we be! There were even more electrical problems with lighting. Brigid had planned to have a set of three spotlights for the food preparation area of the kitchen and it was only when the switch was flicked that it dawned on us that the lighting wasn't so much subtle as non-existent. Our spark, Billy, explained that using the existing electrical set-up meant that only 20 watts reached each spotlight. The actual amount of light emitted was about the same as from a candle.

With everyone else tied up, Billy was left with the major electrical task, leaving the poor chap not so much in his element, but in his own power-less hell. It's this sort of thing that earns him the title of Prince of Darkness. It was handy then, that Graham and his 16-year-old daughter, Bridie, were available to help out elsewhere, with Bridie concentrating on the soft furnishings. Everything fell into place slowly and as for Bob and Brigid, well, it comes as no surprise that they had a few differing opinions concerning work unit shapes.

Billy needed to go back and totally re-wire the whole set-up, changing the transformer and upping the wattage to 150 between the three lights. We didn't really know what the end result would be until night set in, but luckily the moment of truth came and hallelujah! There was light. We even added a dimmer knob for effect.

Jane returned and joined Graham and Bridie in a group hug. She had branded Graham a 'DIY dyslexic', but now he's got the inspiration (and also the accuracy) to finish off the rest of the house – and hopefully, without wonky doors or electrical worries.

Step by Step

Fitting A Dimmer Switch

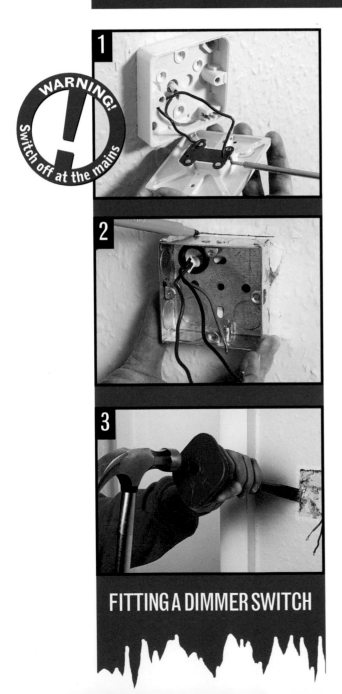

WARNING! Switch off at the mains

Step 1

To ensure the circuit is dead, first turn the light on before switching off at the main fuse box. If supplied, read the manufacturer's instructions for the switch. Using an electricians screwdriver, remove the old switch plate and surface box to free the wires.

Step 2

Punch out an entry hole in the new metal mounting and then fit a rubber grommet (a ring that lines a hole to protect electric cable from chafing). Pass the wires through, position and mark around the box onto the wall.

Step 3

Using a masonry bit, carefully drill around the square to the required depth. Chisel out the waste plaster and brickwork, taking care to avoid the electric cable.

FITTING A DIMMER SWITCH

Step 4

When the box is sitting flush with the surrounding wall, use wall plugs and screws to secure it firmly in place.

Step 5

Make good the rough edge around the box with filler. Now wire in the new dimmer, observing the correct wiring connections suitable to the new switch.

Step 6

Push the switch back into the box and (to avoid causing any damage to the decorative fascia) carefully screw the face plate into position. To test the circuit, switch on the main supply.

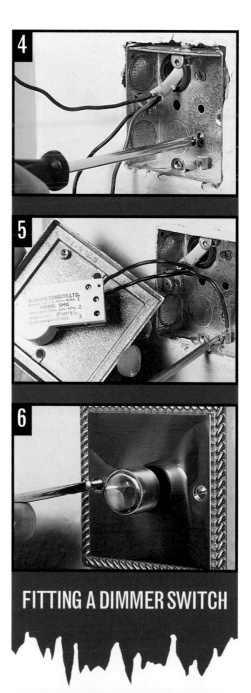

FITTING A DIMMER SWITCH

Step by Step

Fitting Halogen Ceiling Lights

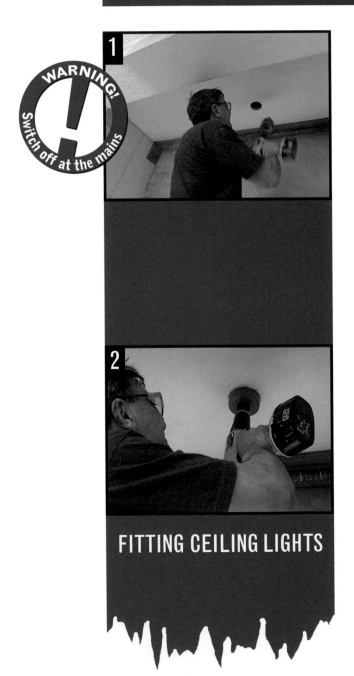

WARNING!
Switch off at the mains

FITTING CEILING LIGHTS

Step 1

Decide how many lights you are going to need, then measure and mark their positions out evenly across the ceiling. Make a tiny hole in the ceiling at each intended location and then check from above that the position is free from any existing wiring or solid obstructions. It is possible to cut out the holes by hand with a padsaw (designed for cutting holes in panels), but even for a short run of lights the use of a holesaw drill attachment will greatly ease the task and very probably give you a much neater finish into the bargain.

Step 2

Once you have selected the correct size of holesaw to suit your chosen light fitting, hold the drill firmly with both hands. Using a slow speed to start with, gradually drill through into the ceiling void. Always wear protective glasses and prepare for dust and debris on removal of the drill.

Step 3

Once all the holes are cut and clean, you can then start to wire up the lights according to the instructions supplied by the manufacturer. Always make sure you have turned the power off at the main fusebox before you attempt this; simply turning the lighting circuit off at the wall switch is not sufficient. Where possible, aim to work from a comfortable height by running longer cable from the ceiling than you might think necessary.

Step 4

Once the wiring process is complete, offer up each fitting into the holes you have cut and then press the light flush to the ceiling (normally a spring loaded clip will hold it in place once you have done this). Reconnect the mains power supply and switch on. You may well find that fitting a dimmer switch will prolong the life of your bulbs. See pages 84–5 for instructions on this procedure.

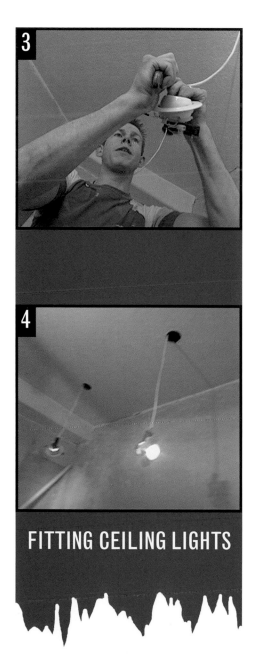

FITTING CEILING LIGHTS

Woodwork

Working with wood is a privilege, and just because it's pretty cheap this doesn't mean it's not capable of the most fantastic results. Wood is strong, flexible, easy to work with, forgiving when you go wrong and hugely rewarding when you get it right. In this section of the book we'll be dealing with most of the instances involving the existing wooden parts of your house (the floors, stairs, doors and window frames), and helping you through most of the techniques needed to keep that wood working well and looking good. Plus, along the way you will begin to see that once you have the right equipment and the right information there are all manner of projects you could undertake with relative ease. If you can make a shelf then you can probably create a new storage box for the kids' room. And if you can make that box, you can probably make a bench, which means you could easily tackle a new bed or even a dining table. Seriously, this stuff is straightforward, common-sense construction technique. Buy a few quality tools, brush up on some simple skills, be prepared to invest the energy and the patience it takes to get things right and you will be amazed at what you can achieve.

'Act naturally,' says Lowri.

'Feel free to experiment with timber and don't worry too much about the cost because if you are going to paint any finished constructions it seems a lot can be done with relatively cheap materials such as MDF.'

One of the best things about *DIY SOS* is that we get to meet all sorts of different people. Still, if the people vary, there are some attitudes to DIY which are common to all of them. One is that DIY is really only about fixing broken things or redecorating others that are dull. Most people tend to draw the line at actually making something new. Before we started the first series I was pretty much of the same opinion. But that was before I met Steve the handyman and discovered wood.

Every show we do, it always amazes me what ingenious constructions can be made from this stuff. And with all the man-made products that are now dominating the DIY market it's quite refreshing to use a natural material. Whether you are putting in a new interior wall, erecting a new shelf or just sanding down the floorboards, wood is still one of the most adaptable and practical materials around.

Now, at my girls' school we didn't do woodwork so I was a bit stumped initially. The trick, I've learned, is not to think of timber as a solid, shapeless slab, but as modelling clay just waiting for you to begin experimenting with it. When making a kitchen work unit, for

Bob the builder: his golden rule is always think a job through before you start.

example, you don't have to stop at being functional. With a little flair it can be turned into something unique and definitely not available from any standard flatpack kitchen supplier.

As a showcase of just what can be achieved when wood is used creatively, in Series Two we turned a dowdy old hall in Walsall into a very impressive and practical entrance, using bare wooden banisters, mirror frames and plain furniture to create a rustic, textured feel, with few other frills necessary to complete the appearance of the room.

Feel free to experiment with a range of different timbers in your own home. Remember, if you are going to paint any finished constructions, a lot can be done with relatively cheap materials such as MDF. A safety tip, though, sawing MDF creates a lot of fine dust. You should always wear a safety mask suitable for MDF and, if you can, cut it outside. Also, as I often have to remind Steve, the correct measurements are vital for success. I'll never forget a man called Maurizio who, when making a dog kennel, muddled his feet with his metres and ended up in the dog house himself. (There was plenty of room for the dog, too.) Oops!

Tools & Materials

In woodwork half the trick is holding everything rigid while you cut or drill; the other half is making sure you are cutting or drilling in the right place.

▶ Possibly the most useful powertool you will ever own (see pages 18 and

▲ If you need to 'encourage' your timber into position, then use a mallet, and ideally a protective scrap of wood between the two.

▶ Get a decent retractable metal rule that is robust and accurate.

▲ Perfect for marking accurate measurement points, starting off screw holes and even scoring lines across the timber.

◀ Buy wood glue and follow the manufacturer's instructions.

▲ The square: perfect for making accurate, 90-degree cuts across lengths of timber.

▲ The tenon saw has a rigid spine along the back of the blade to make sure that every cut you make with it is absolutely straight.

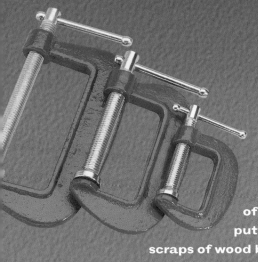

◀ Make sure you protcct the surface of your timber by putting little scraps of wood between these clamps and whatever they are holding.

▲ The modern workbench is a brilliant way to support and secure your project as you mark, cut and assemble everything into place.

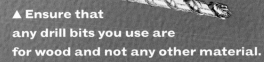

▲ Ensure that any drill bits you use are for wood and not any other material.

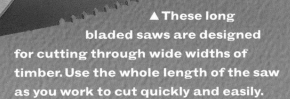

▲ These long bladed saws are designed for cutting through wide widths of timber. Use the whole length of the saw as you work to cut quickly and easily.

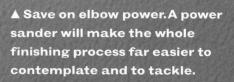

◀ Chisels are designed for chopping out small sections of wood, like a rebate for a door hinge. Punches are used with a hammer to knock nail heads into the wood and out of sight.

▲ Save on elbow power. A power sander will make the whole finishing process far easier to contemplate and to tackle.

7-PIECE CHISEL AND PUNCH SET

Getting Started

While modern houses are constructed with timber that has been impregnated with all manner of chemicals to keep it free from bugs and rot, a lot of older properties don't enjoy this kind of protection. Of the three main enemies to the timber in your home, none are particularly pleasant but some are easier to get rid of than others. Easiest of them all is probably woodworm, which has to have been going on undiscovered for several years before it warrants replacing the affected timber. Telltale tiny holes all over your furniture or floors will warn you of attack, and a prod with a sharp knife will tell you how bad that attack really is. If the wood is still solid and resists the knife, then it's merely a question of spraying everything that's infested with the right chemicals. Your local DIY store or hire shop should be able to advise you here. If the wood crumbles away where the blade of the knife goes in, you've got problems, and if the wood you are testing is loadbearing in any way, floor joists for example, you have bigger problems still. All the affected timber needs to be replaced and the area treated with an insecticide.

Second on the list is wet rot. Timber needs to be dry, with a good circulation of air around it. If the wood in your house gets too damp (see doors and windows most often) then wet rot may arrive. On discovery, find out why that wood is getting wet and stop it happening. Once the moisture level goes down, the rot will stop spreading, but you still need to treat the affected timber. As before, really bad damage has to be cut out and replaced, but minor damage can usually be remedied by a large dose of some chemical wet rot eradicator. Once fixed and dosed, make sure the area remains permanently dry.

Finally, the worst of the bunch: dry rot. Encouraged by damp, but not nearly so dependent on it as wet rot, dry rot can spread at an alarming pace once it has a hold of your woodwork – even through brick. Dry rot is sometimes hard to spot because of where it grows, but it's impossible to mistake once you have found it. If you have pancake-shaped growths or cotton wool covered tubules, get a specialist round to the house pronto and track down every direction in which the dry rot fungus has spread. Cut out everything which offends you and spray everything else. Finally, track down the source of the original dampness, which would have triggered the dry rot, and make sure nothing like this ever happens in your house again.

Step by Step

Woodwork Joints

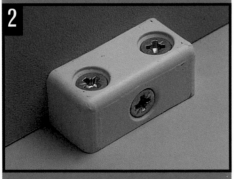

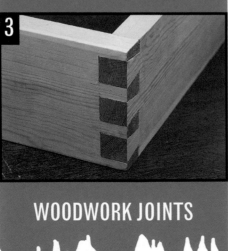

Step 1

Traditional cabinetmaking techniques have, in the main, been replaced by new fixings such as plastic blocks, corner joints, metal brackets, etc. Electric tools and the expense of fine timber has lead to an even greater reduction of finished woodwork.

Step 2

Cabinets and shelving can be built using plastic corner blocks and shelf supports needing only a few screws to secure. Specifically designed hinges are available for man-made boards (left), and having boards cut to size in store ensures square ends.

Step 3

The basic timber joints used in light framework and boxing-in panels rely on square-cut ends to improve joint strength. A mitresaw will guarantee this and will enable you to cut perfect angles.

WOODWORK JOINTS

Step 4

The most commonly used joint in light frame construction is a butt joint (right). Simply bring the two square ends together with a dab of wood glue. Drive in two nails at a slight angle to each other to secure.

Step 5

When fixing two pieces together, where access through the frame is denied, fix with two nails from each side (skew nailing). Temporarily nail a block to one side to stop the joint moving as you drive in the first two nails from the other side.

Step 6

To join two pieces of wood that cross each other and need to stay flat, make a cross halving joint with a saw and chisel. The cut in each piece is half its thickness. A neatly-cut joint will not require fixings, just glue and clamp together until the glue is dry.

WOODWORK JOINTS

Joanna

Now, that is what I call a happy customer... Joanna was brimming with enthusiasm and excitement when *DIY SOS* paid her a visit in her Watford home. The front of Joanna's house was sporting a rotten window that had been causing neighbourhood embarrassment for some time. Joanna's next-door neighbour even went as far as to tell us that the very sight of Joanna's window was 'bloody awful'. We couldn't have this – poor Joanna was to go out in disguise no more. Call out the house medics!

Our team was confident that with Joanna's house we were dealing with a one-day project, and thought that the neighbourhood consensus to rip out the century-old window and then replace it with a shiny modern PVC effort was highly unnecessary. First things first, and Joanna gave us a hand by stripping the window bare with paint remover so we could see the extent of the decay. Always watch your hands when using paint remover as it can be scary stuff that doesn't

spot the difference between old paint and skin. Ouch!

Garfield felt most passionately about the window and he set to work removing the old rotten wood and replacing it with new, retaining the classic shape and structure of the window and supporting the (tiny) sections of existing healthy wood.

The bay window that we were to restore could be opened with a vertical sliding mechanism, something that the poor thing hadn't done properly in a while. After restoring the moving section, Steve came up with some ingenuity that apparently makes the thing slide up and down a lot easier: What you do, after any dirt and dust

has been wiped from the sides of the section, is to rub a block of beeswax on the wood to give it a natural glide once the window is in place. We were all dead impressed by this until Steve added: 'This could, of course, be absolute nonsense, but it works for me.' Cheers, Steve!

And that was that. The window was in place, and the pulley mechanism was restored, a coat of paint added and to finish off, a touch of cream window cleaner, a quick rub down and there you have it.

'My heart just soars! This is fantastic!' Joanna beamed, always able to come up trumps with an appreciative reaction.

Even the neighbours were quite impressed – after hanging around and peeking through curtains all day to see what was going on, they all gathered round for the grand unveiling and they were gob-smacked by the results.

Step by Step

Fitting A Dado or Picture Rail

Step 1

Use a spirit level to mark a horizontal line around the room. Cut the longest length of moulding first, making 45-degree angle cuts into the corners. A handsaw and mitre block is useful for this job. However, access to an electric mitresaw will ease the task.

Step 2

Make sure you check each cut length carefully to ensure a neat fit and then apply two continuous beads of panel adhesive along the back of the moulding.

Step 3

Ideally two people should now press and hold the dado in position. The dado is then secured to the wall with nails to keep it in place while the adhesive sets.

FITTING A DADO RAIL

Step 4

Continue working around the room, fitting one length at a time. Leave everything overnight to allow the adhesive to set hard before applying decorator's filler into any gaps.

Step 5

It is very important to paint knotting solution over the bare wood knots. This helps to prevent any resinous sap bleeding through at a later stage – usually after you have spent all day decorating.

Step 6

To finish, paint one or two coats of wood primer/undercoat to all new timber before applying a coloured top coat of your choice.

FITTING A DADO RAIL

Step by Step

Tongue and Groove Wall Cladding

TONGUE AND GROOVE

Step 1

Fix a series of horizontal battens across the wall at 500mm intervals (clear of pipes or cables) using wall plugs and countersunk screws. Leave a 3mm gap around all the edges to allow for expansion. Where possible, cut several tongue and groove lengths together to speed up the process.

Step 2

Check vertical alignment with a spirit level before nailing the first length up by fixing through the face of the timber onto the battens. Continue by 'secret nailing' at an angle (skew nailing) into the tongue of the boards so the nail heads are hidden when the groove of the next piece is slotted over. You could always use a nail punch to drive home the head of each nail to ensure it lies flush with the timber.

Step 3

Use a hammer and a short off-cut of batten to tap each new length of board into place as you work across the wall. The last piece will probably require cutting to the correct width and securing with nails through the face, as with the first length.

Step 4

For additional rigidity, the top and bottom of the panelling can also be nailed through the face as this part of the boards is usually covered by skirting and moulding. Fill any visible nail heads with a natural coloured filler once all the cladding is complete.

Step 5

Where nailing proves difficult, use panel adhesive to ease the job and finally, remember to apply knotting solution to the exposed knots before applying at least two coats of clear varnish, or even wood stain.

TONGUE AND GROOVE

Step by Step

Hanging A Door

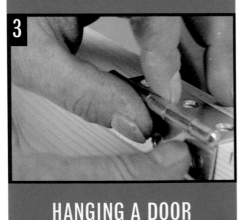

HANGING A DOOR

Step 1

If necessary, cut the new door to the required length using a handsaw or hire an electric circular saw. Trim the sides with a woodplane, leaving a 3mm gap all the way around and sand all edges before continuing.

Step 2

Use wedges at the base to help you hold the door centrally against the frame and then mark off the existing hinge positions with a sharp pencil.

Step 3

Hold the hinge in place against the door and mark the edges with a pencil mark. Also establish the thickness of the hinge on the face of the door. You can score these marks with a craft knife, which will significantly improve the accuracy of the following step.

Step 4

Take a chisel and tap along the marked lines, then neatly pare away the waste until the hinge sits flush in the recess.

Step 5

Hold the door firmly and screw each hinge into position. You need only use one screw at this stage, but make sure it goes in far enough to sit flush with the surface of the hinge.

Step 6

Lift the door into position (use wedges if necessary). Screw the door hinges onto the frame and check it closes properly. Adjust the position of the hinges by loosening the single screw securing them to the door. Finally, insert the remaining screws to secure.

HANGING A DOOR

Step by Step

Sanding Floors

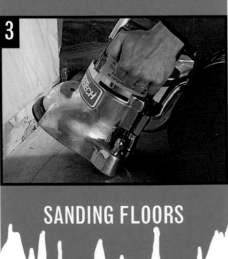

Step 1

Sanding a floor is a fairly simple job, but it creates a lot of dust. Seal off the door to the room and always wear a dust mask. Punch down protruding nail heads below the surface. When hiring sanding equipment, ask for advice on how to use it and what grades of sanding belts you need.

Step 2

Start at the edge of the room and work along the length of the boards, keeping the sander away from the skirting boards to avoid damage. Repeat the process with medium and fine sanding belts until a narrow border remains all around the room.

Step 3

Strip the remaining border using an edge sander. Carefully work around the edge, avoiding the paintwork. When finished, vacuum the whole area a few times before wiping the boards with a slightly damp cloth to finish. The floor is now ready for varnishing.

SANDING FLOORS

Step by Step

Curing Creaking Floorboards

Step 1

Follow the board along to establish the nearest cut end, then start there by hammering a bolster chisel into the gap and levering up the board edge. Work on both sides of the board until you're able to wedge a claw hammer under the edge to aid the process of lifting the board.

Step 2

Once you have lifted one end completely clear of the floor, slide the chisel underneath so it sits across two neighbouring boards. Now stand on the lifted end to prise up more of the board. Continue working along by sliding the chisel further and further.

Step 3

Once the board is completely free, remove all the old nails and screw it back down into position. Take careful note of any plumbing pipes or electric cables which might be lurking under the floor (you do not want to put a screw through one of these!).

CURING CREAKS

Step by Step

Laying A Laminate Floor

Step 1

Remove floor coverings. Fix loose boards and hammer down any nails. If necessary, nail down 6mm plywood sheets. Remove skirting or plan to fit a matching decorative wooden bead or 'quadrant' to cover 10mm expansion gaps which must be left at the edges.

Step 2

Roll out the foam underlay against the longest wall. Lay the laminate boards down with the groove facing the skirting. The first row of boards must be accurately positioned parallel to the wall. To check, set out a dry run of boards before securing anything.

Step 3

Cut the last board (handsaw or jigsaw) of the first row into position and (if over 300mm) use the off-cut to start the next row. After three rows, check the whole alignment. When correct, remove the boards, apply wood glue into the grooves and relay everything.

LAYING A LAMINATE FLOOR

Step 4

Make sure you maintain the important 10mm expansion gap from all wall edges. Each board should be tapped together using a hammer and wooden block to ensure the gap is closed. As each gap is closed, any excess glue should be cleaned away immediately.

Step 5

Having laid the three initial rows, allow the glue to dry for about two hours to ensure a sound base, preventing alignment and joint gap problems later. Continue to lay the remaining boards by glueing each one as you work across to the opposite wall.

Step 6

The last row may need to be cut along its length before slotting into position, but don't forget the 10mm expansion gap where it meets the wall. Finally, refit the skirting or nail the matching quadrant to the skirting so that all the expansion gaps are covered.

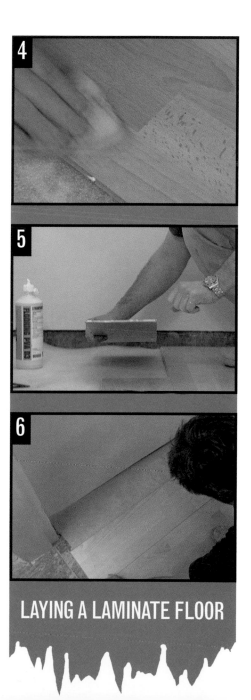

LAYING A LAMINATE FLOOR

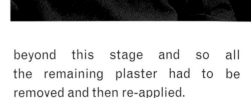

Barry & Andrea

If you are one of those people who couldn't resist the charm of an old house when you were looking round the estate agents, then you will undoubtedly already know all the problems a classic building brings with it. One of the most common is damp – a condition known all too well by Barry and Andrea, the couple we visited in Runcorn.

Their house had been devastated by rising damp, which had climbed high up the walls, drawing moisture away from internal plastering and so causing it to crumble away. Usually, rising damp can be treated successfully at an early stage by drilling holes into the wall at ground level and then injecting silicon into the brickwork, forming a waterproof layer that repels any damp. Sadly, the walls had dampened

beyond this stage and so all the remaining plaster had to be removed and then re-applied.

This really was a task that tested our team to the limits, especially as Andrea laid down some strict rules about how the house should look. Brigid was upset by this, particularly with the lovely old bay window that Andrea wished us to replace with new. It featured charming latticed stained glass, but sadly it had to all come out. We did, however, recycle the glass.

One tip worth remembering when removing glass from windows is to stick masking tape across the window so that it is almost totally covered. When you give the pane a firm tap in the middle the glass falls out in a lump without shattering, being held together by the tape. Remember to wrap the glass in paper though, to avoid cutting anyone.

Andrea and Barry had already bought the

material they wanted for the laminate flooring. Unfortunately, however, it was not the best quality for the job in hand, being made of plastic-coated MDF. The problem with this stuff is that though it looks great for the first few months, if anything sharp and heavy is dropped on it, the plastic gets punctured and the MDF shows through. Your only choice then is to get a decent rug and cover it up, which is hardly an ideal option.

Part of our success with this project was Barry. Although he's a milkman and has to get up ridiculously early, he still managed to return after his round, help us decorate and get enough kip for his round.

As it was an old house, we decided to put some coving up in the dining room in order to hide any gaps and cracks that might appear between the wall and ceiling.

After damp-proofing the front room, we had to leave the plaster to dry for a couple of weeks before painting it, but the dining room was decorated up a treat. What made it extra special was that it was Andrea's birthday, so our team even had time to scrub the paint off their hands and make a birthday cake for her.

We knew that Andrea was a tough cookie to please, but when she saw what we had done she burst into tears... of joy, thankfully!

Top Tips

From the DIY SOS website www.bbc.co.uk/homes

Skirting Board

If your skirting board has a gap between it and the floor, put another board on top of it and gently push down with your leg. When the gap has disappeared, secure the skirting board in this position.

How To Use A Saw

To saw a true square edge, just look down your saw so you can see both sides of the teeth. Then you will know the saw is plumb and, if you keep watching it as you saw, you'll find you always saw a straight, true line.

To Start A Screw

First, hammer in a small nail where you want the screw to go, but make sure you don't hammer it in all the way. Using pliers, remove the nail and – hey, presto! – you have the perfect entry for your screw. Points to remember: use a nail that is quite a bit slimmer than the screw size and don't hammer it all the way in!

To Stop Wood Splitting

Turn the nail over and then tap the point gently with a hammer. This produces a blunt point which won't follow the natural grain of the timber and so the wood won't split.

Share your views with DIY friends on our website!

Small Nails

Do you need to hammer in small nails or pins? Use a comb to hold them in place and you can avoid hammering your fingers.

Decorating

Everybody wants their home to look just right, and there has never been a better time to change the existing look of your house. There has never been a bigger choice of colours and patterns in DIY shops, a better selection of magazines and TV programmes to inspire you, and there has never been a better range of foolproof tools and materials with which to work. But if you don't actually know how to paint properly or how to hang paper correctly, all that money's going to be wasted on a job that never looks quite right. Decorating has always been a big factor with *DIY SOS*, and rightly so. However much you may want to admire your new brickwork or marvel at your plastering technique, there comes a time when you need to finish it all off in a way that does you proud. In this section of the book we've gone back to basics to give you a solid grounding in the tricks and techniques you need to know before tackling any painting, papering or tiling project. There's nothing very complicated to learn. Like everything on the programme, it's all pretty much common sense. However, once you have the basic techniques safely under your belt, then you really can start to work magic.

'Let's create,' says Lowri.

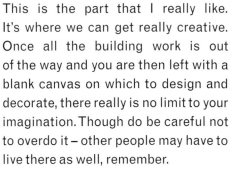

'If you want to amaze your neighbours with the latest schemes, check out the home magazines — that's what Brigid does!'

This is the part that I really like. It's where we can get really creative. Once all the building work is out of the way and you are then left with a blank canvas on which to design and decorate, there really is no limit to your imagination. Though do be careful not to overdo it – other people may have to live there as well, remember.

The first thing to remember is that there are no real right or wrong ways to decorate. If you like the end results, it's right. But if you don't, it's probably wrong, but always fixable. And don't be intimidated by the size of the task. You'll be amazed how much wall you can cover with a pot of paint, a roller and an afternoon to spare. Our team once visited a woman called Jacqui and in just three days, we totally redecorated her house from top to bottom. Rope in some of the family to help out and you can achieve similar results, though you might want to consider some of the lessons we have learnt along the way...

Brigid's wonderful watercolour room plans are not just for show; they are there to help co-ordinate the team and act as a guide for Brigid, so that she knows which colours go where and

Brigid the decorator: her golden rule is to start and finish one room at a time.

Bob knows exactly what he's letting himself in for on each programme.

If you are going for the modern look and want to amaze your neighbours with the latest schemes, then check out home magazines for up- to-the-minute ideas (that's what Brigid does). Otherwise, let your imagination run wild. If you want to give a plain wall the personal touch, why not try a stencil, or even cover one side of a shaped sponge in paint and dab it on the wall. If you fancy yourself as an artist, murals can be great fun for kids' bedrooms and you can even let the kids join in the fun. And it might just stop them from totally covering the

walls in their David Beckham or 5ive posters into the bargain.

I can recall the time when the team decorated the huge former recreation room of a fire station, that was in a terrible state, and transformed it into a community room. Here, Brigid used a technique to blend two wall colours together by placing them in stripes in the roller tray and giving the roller a two-tone covering. The resulting wall was deep blue at the bottom, light blue at the top, with the middle blending together in a lovely gradient.

Finally, I can also remember a cry for help that we answered when we visited a poor girl named Cindy. Her ex-boyfriend had tried to turn her home into a 'gothic mansion', but cut some corners when it came to the bathroom. He painted everything – and I mean everything – totally black, even the sink and loo, inside and out. Cindy was tempted to offer guests a bucket in the garden instead of a visit to her black hole of a bathroom. Now that's what you call an (in)convenience.

Tools & Materials

The problem with decorating is that everything tends to get very messy very quickly. So clean everything off after each job, or the tools will be useless by the time you need them next.

▲ If you are prepared to clean up afterwards, you can also use your scraper as an emergency filler knife as well.

▶ You need two brushes when wallpapering. One to apply the adhesive and one to rub over the surface of the paper when it's up to remove any bubbles. Don't mix them up!

▲ Get a decent retractable metal rule that is robust and accurate.

▲ Tempting as the dining room table is, a proper wallpapering table specially designed for the job is not only going to make the whole process easier, it will actually make it quicker, too.

▲ You can get just about every type of paint you need in water-based formulations, some of which give off perfumed aromas as they dry.

▲ Not only will a roller apply paint faster than any brush could ever do, it also does it without leaving any tell-tale brush marks in the finish.

▲ A sharp knife and long rule are the best way to apply straight and accurate cuts to wallpaper. You don't get these with a pair of scissors.

► Cheap brushes are a waste of money. The bristles just clog up and fall out. Get some quality brushes in a variety of sizes.

◄ Use only a proper, stable stepladder when working at height.

Getting Started

The first thing you will notice as you flick through the pages that follow is that you have to go about a dozen pages in before anybody starts to decorate anything. This is a reflection on how important it is to get the basics of your decorating right before you rush into the fun bits at the end. If you were making a cake, you wouldn't start off with the icing, would you? Painting a wall doesn't hide the holes that you couldn't be bother to fill, and papering a room doesn't get rid of the lumps of old paper you couldn't be bothered to strip. Preparing to decorate doesn't just mean giving the walls or the woodwork a quick fill and a good rub down. Good decorating needs careful planning and that doesn't start when you come back from the shops, it begins long before you even set off.

First, make sure you are certain about what you are going to do before you do it. The worst time to find that you don't actually like the colours you've chosen is just after you've finished painting the room. Make sure such decisions are the right ones, and that everyone involved agrees on them, too! If you are thinking of re-decorating a room you can do a lot worse than make it all white before painting on some big patches of the colours you are intending to use. Or hang a couple of lengths of the wallpapers you are trying to choose between. Once they're up, leave them there. Leave them so that you can find out how they look in the afternoon sun, how they look in electric light at night and even, after a couple of weeks, whether you still actually like them at all. Once you are sure you have picked the right paint or paper, then and only then, move on to stage two.

You now need to work out exactly how much of your chosen stuff you are going to need, and what equipment you'll need to get the job done properly. Coverage for paint and paper is always worked out by square metres, so measure the length and height of all the walls you intend to decorate to work out the area you will need to buy for. Next, work out what else you'll need... How are you going to reach everywhere? Do you need filler and sandpaper to prepare the walls first? What are you going to apply the filler with?

None of this is going to keep you up at night worrying, but all of it is worth thinking about while you have a shopping list in your hand and not a dripping paint brush. That said, the walls await you. Read on...

Step by Step

Stripping Wallpaper

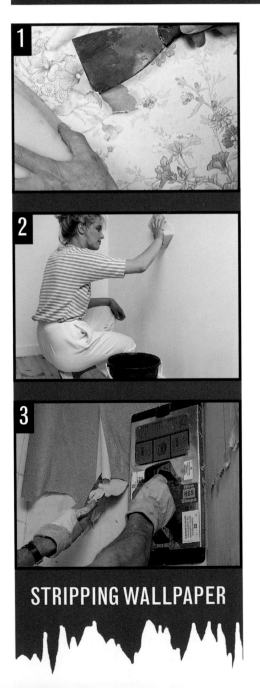

STRIPPING WALLPAPER

Step 1

To remove standard wallpaper, add a little washing-up liquid to a bucket of hot water. Apply it to the wall with a sponge (or use a large garden spray). Leave to soak for a few minutes, then take a wide-bladed stripping knife to lift the softened paper.

Step 2

If the paper has been painted or is heavily layered, then before you soak it, score the surface with the edge of a filling knife or craft knife. Take care not to damage the plaster underneath, though. That'd mean more work later.

Step 3

To save time and energy when you are stripping large or difficult areas, hire a steam stripper. To speed up the process further, keep the plate in contact with the next part of the wall while you strip the soaked paper from the area already treated.

Step by Step

Preparing Walls

Step 1

Having removed all the old wallpaper, the wall will need further preparation before painting or papering begins. Small cracks are best channelled out into a 'V' shape using the edge of a filling knife or specialised tool. Brush out the crack first to remove any dust.

Step 2

Damp down the groove with a wet brush before mixing up the filler to a thick paste (if not ready mixed). Using a wide filling knife, press the filler into the crack. Finish off with one long stroke to smooth the filler out, but leave it slightly raised on the surface.

Step 3

When completely dry, sand the filler level to the wall with a sandpaper block or electric pad sander. Fill cracks in corners, or gaps between walls and skirting, with decorator's chalk filler from a tube and gun. Lightly sand the wall and seal with PVA solution.

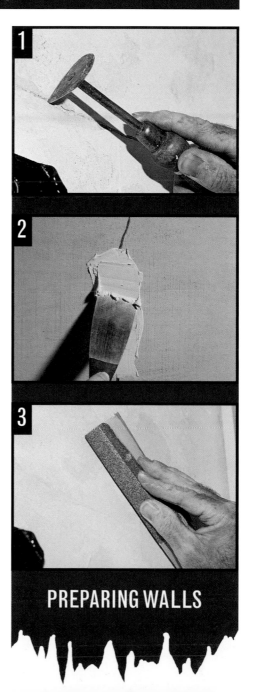

PREPARING WALLS

Step by Step

Using A Paint Roller

USING A PAINT ROLLER

Step 1

Rollers are an ideal alternative to paint brushes, particularly for walls and ceilings. Various roller 'sleeves' are available; choose 'short pile' sleeves for smooth surfaces and oil paints, 'medium pile' for most emulsion work, and 'long pile' for painting heavily textured surfaces.

Step 2

Having 'cut in' (painted) all the outside edges of your walls with a small brush beforehand, pour a small amount of paint into the tray reservoir. Dip the roller into it and then rub it lightly over the ribbed area of the tray to spread an even amount over the entire sleeve.

Step 3

Aim to keep the roller in contact with the wall the whole time and use random strokes to spread an even amount of paint into a rough square block. Finish off by using light vertical movements, then reload the roller with paint and continue across the wall.

Step 4

Most of the modern rollers will also accept extension handles or poles that allow you to reach inaccessible areas or to paint the ceiling without having to use stepladders or erect a time-consuming work platform.

Step 5

To make painting behind the radiators easier, try using a specially designed 'radiator roller', which has a long handle and a very slim roller sleeve. You can also get short 100mm foam rollers, which are ideal for painting oil-based paints onto radiator panels.

Step 6

When the job is complete you can scrape excess paint off the roller with a flat-bladed filling knife. Roll the remaining paint out onto scrap paper and then remove the sleeve to give it a final rinse under warm water.

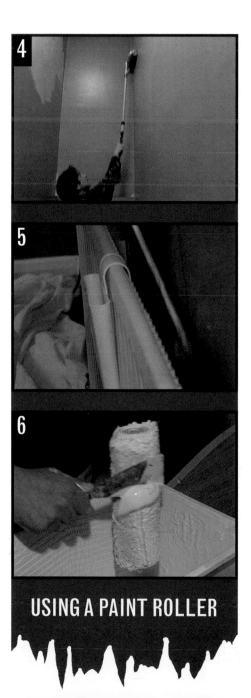

USING A PAINT ROLLER

Caro & Rob

The first thing a guest sees when you invite them into your home is the entrance hall. Apparently, a lot of people lay their hallway with a red carpet to create an instant grand effect, because it's an old and often true saying that first impressions last.

We pitied Caro in her Walsall home when she told us of the grief her hallway was giving her. She told me: 'I open the front door and people say "Have you just moved in?" and I say, "No, we've been here nine years!" And her partner Rob is a builder and plumber by trade too! But he's far too interested in his motorbike to worry. That can be the problem with activities as enjoyable as DIY – when Rob's fun-hobby view of the trade was taken away and it became a profession, his home improvement get-up-and-go had got-up-and-gone.

This house was one of our easiest clean-up jobs, with

stair banisters so wobbly you could yank them out by hand. We decided to be ruthless and to remove the entire banister, not just the spindle. Sometimes a ruthless attitude can be handy – restoring existing décor when appropriate saves money – but sometimes you have to start afresh.

Replacing banisters is a lot easier than you might think and you can buy a complete baserail and handrail set already marked to show exactly where the spindles go.

To make a change, Brigid decided she would use wallpaper here instead of paint. She wanted to give the hallway a rustic feel, with lots of bare wood and subtly-patterned lavender wallpaper.

There was some drama when a lack of correct maths from

Brigid resulted in a hallway mirror ending up too big to fit in the frame Bob made. Brigid's advice was to 'Just cut it', which is easier said than done. Rob took a Stanley knife and (using a ruler) made a straight incision across the mirror. You only get one chance at doing this, as you can't come back and cut again. Then gently tap along the back of the incision, watching the pressure lines form on the glass, before, with a little bit of skillful luck, the mirror separates. The suspense nearly killed us.

Once the ceiling had been rubbed down and painted, the wallpaper was applied. There were few team conflicts this time, though builder Bob was a bit cheeky when he ventured off on his own and bought a door with handles without Brigid's consent. She wasn't too chuffed. Bob made it up to her later on by finishing with enough time to spare to build a telephone seat and table around an ugly gas meter, adding a hinged lid to keep it accessible.

The wallpaper gave the hallway a texture and uniqueness, with very few frills. Caro was stunned by the results and could be proud that Rob had torn himself away from his motorbike for long enough to give our lot a helping hand.

Step by Step

Preparing And Painting Woodwork

PREPARING WOODWORK

Step 1

Paintwork in bad condition requires removal to be lasting and smooth. To clear off old paint, use a hot air gun (see manufacturer's instructions) to soften it and then scrape along with a shave hook to scratch the surface back to the original bare timber.

Step 2

All rotten exterior wood needs to be chopped back to a sound base and then treated with a 'paint on' wood hardener combined with a two-part resin based wood filler. This is a highly effective alternative to completely replacing the woodwork.

Step 3

Once filled and treated, use abrasive paper to sand down all the repaired areas and surrounding woodwork until completely smooth. Dust off and wipe over with a slightly damp cloth. When everything is dry, apply two coats of wood primer undercoat to all areas.

Step 4

Always brush knotting solution over any resin soaked areas or knots, as the sap can later bleed through your finished paintwork. Once the knotting solution is completely dry, you can then apply two coats of primer undercoat as before.

Step 5

Use a hand-held paint shield or apply masking tape for a really neat finish on windows. Paint onto the glass window pane by about 3mm as this creates a seal between the glass and frame. This is particularly important when you are working on the exterior of windows.

Step 6

The small knocks and chips which often occur around the bottom of door frames and along the skirting are best touched in using a small artist's brush. You can also use this technique to improve the appearance of your interior woodwork.

PAINTING WOODWORK

Step by Step

Spray Etching On Glass

SPRAY ETCHING GLASS

Step 1

Draw a rough version of your intended design on paper. Wipe your surface with methylated spirit before applying the sticky-back plastic that will act as a mask for your design. You can even use parcel tape for this if you don't have any self-adhesive plastic film.

Step 2

Use a pen to redraw your paper design onto the plastic covering, then take a craft knife and cut it out. Starting at the highest point of your design, apply light, even strokes of 'spray etch'. Leave five minutes between coats and keep applying the etch as required.

Step 3

When the desired finish is achieved, leave the work until fully dry. You can then carefully lift up an edge of the remaining plastic film and peel it all away to expose the finished design.

Step by Step

Fitting Plaster Coving

Step 1

Remove loose plaster (if bare, prime with PVA). Score painted surfaces. Now erect a solid and safe platform. On the longest run of wall, use a 'coving mitre template' (right) to saw away a 45-degree angle from the end of the first length of coving. If it is too long, cut down and mitre the other end.

Step 2

Mix the adhesive. Work from both ends towards the middle, applying adhesive along the flat strips on the back of the coving. Lift coving into position and with one uniform movement, press firmly into position and keep applying pressure for a least one minute.

Step 3

Continue fitting one length of coving at a time. Remove any excess adhesive with a filling knife after each one is fitted. Using a wet, old paintbrush, smooth over the joints ready for painting. Leave large (5mm) gaps between each one and then finish off with filler at the end.

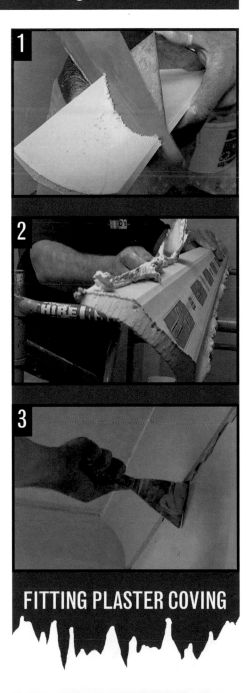

FITTING PLASTER COVING

Step by Step

Hanging Wallpaper

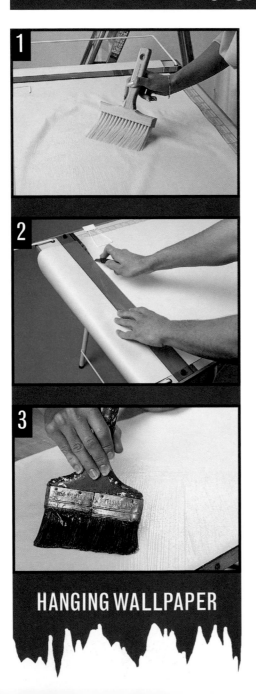

Step 1

These are the basic steps to hanging lining paper. This is the best way to build confidence through the practice of handling, cutting and pasting, without matching pattern. The tools are the same for any kind of hanging.

Step 2

Measure the height of the room from the top of the skirting adding 100mm allowing for overlaps top and bottom. Unroll the paper on a pasting table. Measure off and then fold as many lengths as are on the roll. Cut off the lengths with scissors or a knife.

Step 3

Having mixed up a bucket of paste, use a wide brush to line the centre of the paper. Work out from the line in a herringbone pattern to the edges. Keep one edge off the side of the table to avoid getting paste on the face side.

HANGING WALLPAPER

Step 4

Fold the pasted side back together so that the top and bottom ends meet in the middle and leave to soak for 10 minutes. Mark off the width of a roll in the corner of the room. Move 12mm closer to the corner and then mark a vertical line down the wall.

Step 5

Carry the paper to the wall and let a fold drop. Use a brush to slide and position the paper to the line. Start at the top and leave a 50mm overlay where wall meets ceiling or cornice. Brush down the wall and unfold the bottom to overlap the skirting.

Step 6

Use a short stamping motion with the brush to press the paper into the edges for trimming. Crease the paper with the tip of some scissors along the edges. Peel the paper slightly to cut the excess away. Brush to remove air pockets and press down the edges.

HANGING WALLPAPER

Jacqui & Cas

Most of us have at least one dodgy bedroom. Jacqui had five. She had moved into a house which had been repossessed and completely stripped by its previous owner. It 'needed a bit of work'. Although friends promised to give her a helping hand, unfortunately it never happened and she had been living in a mess ever since. Jacqui, a single mum with a day job, says that after work and tidying the devastation of toys the kids have left for her, DIY generally starts at somewhere near midnight, when she's too exhausted to even hold a paintbrush.

We told Jacqui we were just going to concentrate on the hall and stairway, but after we had sent her off, we set about making her the best surprise ever: we were going to decorate the entire house. In three days? We must be mad. But that was our task and it went surprisingly smoothly.

Jacqui's best friend, Cas, was around to help us out and she, being a self-confessed DIY lover, was a great help. Our plasterer, Chris, taught her the ropes, though was slightly confused by the comment she made that lobbing great big lumps of plaster onto a wall is a whole lot like applying make-up. Let's hope it really isn't, Cas.

I'd never seen so much paint and in only two days, the entire house was done, leaving us the remaining day for trimmings. The only conflict Brigid and Bob had this time was resolved in a mature, orderly fashion – they had a paint fight and ended up covered in it.

That old favourite, the shaped sponge pattern, was applied to walls to add a bit of texture, while Brigid showed off her flair for fine art by painting a dolphin wall mural in one of the kids' bedrooms. One other nice effect was carried out on an old downstairs door window: sheets of sticky tape were applied to the glass in

wavy patterns, before the uncovered glass was sprayed with a coat of spray etch. We then peeled the sticky-back plastic off and the areas of sprayed glass were revealed to have a frosty, etched appearance. You can build the sticky tape up and re-spray for a heightened effect. Each of the children's rooms was given a personality of its own using quick and simple techniques.

Once the kids' bedrooms were complete, Brigid went about turning Jacqui's room into a real love-nest. After months of peeling wallpaper and tatty furniture, romantic colour schemes were applied and there were frills galore: the perfect relaxation haven. As Jacqui was led from room to room, she couldn't believe her eyes.

Step by Step

Tiling A Kitchen Splashback

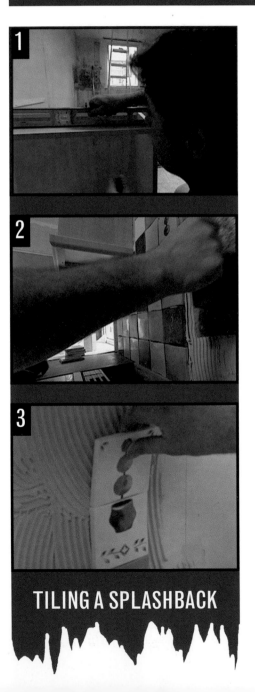

TILING A SPLASHBACK

Step 1

As with all kitchen tiling, check that the work surface is level. If it's not, then pin a level batten to the wall before you start (which is essential anyway for larger areas).

Step 2

Take a notched trowel spreader and apply a horizontal bed of adhesive to a small area of the wall, enough for just a few tiles. Increase the working area as you become more proficient.

Step 3

Using a slight twisting motion, press the tiles into place, covering all the area you have previously covered with your trowel.

Step 4

If required, insert tile spacers between each tile. This will ensure a uniform gap both horizontally and vertically. Finally, remove any excess adhesive around the tiles before starting each new block, leaving all the cuts to last.

Step 5

Use a tile cutter to score and snap the tiles to size, fixing them into position one at a time. When cutting tiles, it's advisable to use one firm scoring action. Eventually this will lead to fewer unwanted breakages. Honest!

Step 6

Having left the tiles to dry overnight, you can start grouting. Using a rubber squeegee, press grout fully into any gaps. Leave a short time before wiping them over with a damp sponge in a circular motion. Finally, remove any dust on the surface with a dry cloth.

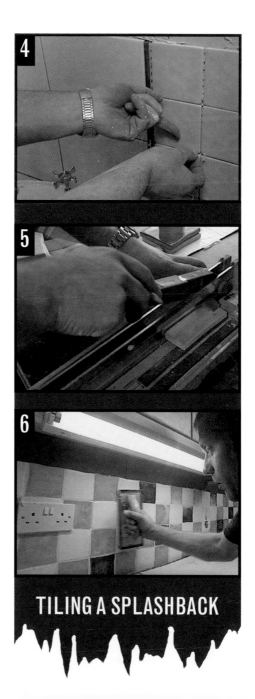

TILING A SPLASHBACK

Top Tips

Paintbrush Tips

Buy the most expensive brush you can, the difference is amazing!

If you are waiting for a coat of (gloss) paint to dry, wrap the business end in clingfilm and it will stop the brush from drying.

Never leave brushes in a jar of liquid. This makes the bristles bend at the tip and you'll never get the brush to lie 'straight' again.

Sheepskin Rollers

It's always worth investing in quality, sheepskin rollers. They will hold the paint a lot better and the paint will go on more easily and evenly, and they'll also last for years if cleaned correctly after use.

Share your views with DIY friends on our website!

Cushion Covers

To change the design of your cushion covers to match your room colour, photocopy your design onto heat transfer paper, then simply iron onto your fabric. You can buy heat transfer paper from most craft shops.

Sticking Laminate

If you want to stick laminate or sheet veneer to, say, a tabletop, apply contact adhesive to both surfaces and wait until touch-dry (not tacky!). Lay sheets of newspaper on the tabletop, leaving just half an inch at one edge exposed. Place laminate, glue-side down, on top of the newspaper and then carefully line up with the receiving surface. When square, press down onto the edge where there's no paper. Then, working slowly, pull out the paper from the opposite edge, carefully smoothing down the laminate as you go along and working outwards from the centre line to avoid air pockets.

Resources

KITCHENS / APPLIANCES

MauriceLay Distribtuors Ltd
0117 9387412
Chippendale Kitchens
01724 276276
www.designacademy.co.uk
Perstorp Surface Materials (UK) Ltd
01325 303303
www.perstorpsurfaces.com
The Shaker Kitchen & Furniture Workshop
01353 721605
J.G Henry Lewis Fitted Furniture
0161 3306000
Waeco International
01305 854000
Lakeland Limited
015394 88100
www.lakelandlimited.com
James Latham
01454 273501
Leisure Consumer Product
0870 7895107
www.leisurecp.co.uk
Orama Fabrications Ltd
01773 521884
www.orama.co.uk
Smeg (UK) Ltd
08708 437373
www.smeguk.com
Trago Mills
01579 348877

FLOORING

Tomkinsons Carpets Ltd
0800 374 429
Duralay Ltd
01706 213131
Florco Wholesalers
01635 864455
Carpet Sense
01702 434134
Diala Carpet
01432 279877
Rapid Hardware
0151 7082037
Brighouse Flooring Co.
01484 401199
Disney Flooring Ltd
01934 615005
Bob Jude Flooring
01633 868976
Responsive Designs
01276 682682
www.responsivedesigns.co.uk
Hyde Flooring Company Ltd
0161 3681851
Harwoods Carpets Ltd
01257 274965
www.steeleylanecarpets.co.uk
Dalsouple
01984 667551
www.dalsouple.co.uk
Uzin Ltd
01235 534106
Wool Classics
0207 3490090

LIGHTING / ELECTRICAL

IBL Lighting
0208 3917500
www.ibl.co.uk
Ring Lighting Plc
0113 2767676
City Electrical Factors
01484 538221
Trident Manufacturing
0808 1009933
Lamplite
01364 653431
www.lamplite.net
Number 1 Lighting
01985 216624
Noral
01908 618181
Independant Lighting Specialist
0161 736 1237
Meredith Electrical Distributors
0161 344 2425
Electrical Wholesale Supplies (Wales) Ltd
01495 725777
Zero 88 Lighting Ltd
01633 838088
www.zero.88.com
Amari Plastics Plc
0117 9723900
Ring Lighting Plc
0113 2767676

PAINT / WALLPAPER

Crown
01254 704951
www.crownpaint.co.uk
www.sandtex.co.uk
Sanderson
01895 201509
Vymura
0800 591984
FADS
01477 544544
www.FADS.co.uk
www.thegismoshop.co.uk
Refina Ltd
01202 632270
www.refina.co.uk
Sika Ltd
01707 394444
Mason Coatings
01332 295959
Dulux Decorating Centre for wallpaper, paint & accessories
0117 9240317

BATHROOM / PLUMBING

Screwfix
0800 317004/0500 414141
www.screwfix.com
Rudge & Co
0121 4402633

FURNISHINGS

Hillarys
0800 716564
www.hillarys.co.uk

BHS
02072623288
Oldrids Department Store
01205 361251
Richer Sounds
0117 9734397

FURNITURE

Paul Milton Woodturning
01364 643722
Spindlewood Woodturning
01278 453666
Stompa Furniture Ltd
01274 596885
www.stompa.co.uk
Jali Ltd (fretwork)
01227 831710
www.jali.co.uk
Furniture Forge
0151 5256644
Drakes Bar Furniture
01484 425007
Reclaimation UK
0117 9279900
Acorn Windows & Doors
01495 717754
Hillswood Aluminium Furniture
01474 854411
JELD-WEN UK Ltd
0800 1383300
Discount Doors & Joinery Ltd
01626 362926

TILES

Tileflair
0117 9526666
The Tile Centre
01708 762671
Fired Earth
01295 814300

BUILDING SUPPLIES

Jewsons Ltd
0800 539766
Graham Group Plc
01626 331024
K.C Skeet Ltd
0113 2744022
Ken Mart Timber & Slate Products
01626 833564
The Cornish Lime Company
01208 79779
J Scadding & Son Ltd
0117 9556032
Elias Wild & Sons
0161 3302214
Refinery Supplies Ltd
0161 627 5223
Doughty Engineering
01425 478961
Richard Rhodes & Partners Ltd
0161 4278388

HIRE EQUIPMENT

HSS Hire Shops
0845 728 2828
www.hss.co.uk
Speedy Hire
01332 380493
Kingfisher Hire & Sales Ltd
01633 875922
Rubicorn Beverages Ltd
01495 712950

WINDOWS / GLAZIERS

The Heritage Sash Window Compar
0800 0832129
Green berg Glass Ltd
02920 363363
Aacme Glass Ltd
01633 244926
Brownhills Glaziers
01543 370238
The Window Warehouse
0151 5211911

SPECIALIST

Philip Watts Design
0115 974809
www.portholes.co.uk
TMC Fireplaces
0151 4480033
Liberon
01797 367555
Bencrete
0161 338 3046
Allcord Ltd
01912 848444
Threadwell Plc
0161 4296205
British Waterways
01606 723866
Grove Products
0161 367717
www.groveproducts.co.uk
Forgetec Engineering
01594 835363

GENERAL

Cheshire Hanging Baskets
0161 330 0986
Secret Garden
01495 785237
Pets Corner
01272 874747
Petsmart
0117 977 3705
Ronseal Limited
0114 2467171
www.ronseal.co.uk

TOOLS / VANS

Bosch
01895 838743
www.bosch.co.uk
DeWALT High Performance Professional Tools & Accessories
0700 4339258
Hilti (GB) Ltd
0800 886100
Vauxhall Vans supplied by Scenario (UK) Ltd
01279 771791
Rapesco
01732 464800
ITW Construction
01792 589 800
Lowe-Alpine UK Ltd
01539 740840
www.loealpine.com
NEXT Plc
0207 499 6517
Debenhams Plc
0207 408 4444